The Magic and Mystery of Dreams:

The Ultimate Handbook
for Interpreting Day and Night Dreams
and the Symbols in Your Life

by

Jean Walters, DM, DD, CRT

The Magic and Mystery of Dreams:
The Ultimate Handbook for Interpreting Day and Night Dreams and the Symbols in Your Life

ISBN-13: 978-0-9979375-3-4

All rights reserved
Copyright © 2020 by Jean Walters

No part of this book may be reproduced without written permission from the publisher or copyright holders, except for a reviewer who may quote brief passages in review; nor may any part of this book be reproduced, stored in a retrieval system, or transmitted in any form or by any means electronic, mechanical, photocopying, recording or other, without written permission from the publisher or copyright holders.

Cover Design by
Cathy Davis
All rights reserved

Published November 2020
Inner Connections Publishing
St. Louis, MO
All Rights Reserved.

Welcome Reader

Thank you for your support in purchasing this book. It is my great joy to share this information with you that you may live an exalted life of freedom and peace.

Please check out my video library on youtube.com, which promises to instruct you in universal laws, meditation techniques, and personal empowerment. By understanding these principles and applying them to your life, you become the master of your destiny and you open to greater and greater possibilities. May you be enriched.

Dedication

I dedicate this book to spiritual adventurers, those who seek after truth knowing all the while that there is a plan in operation in the Universe, and, by gosh, they are bound to discover it. May you recognize a path opening before you as you learn the language of dreams.

Acknowledgement

I live a life of gratitude for all the people who have allowed me to share my message with them and for their willingness to share their dreams and experiences with me. That is what this book is – a compilation of experiences that have brought each person another step closer to his goal of enlightenment and a life rich with possibilities.

I have been honored to work with amazingly talented people. My editor, Anne Cote, has an eagle eye for what needs to be done and the creative ability to not only see the path ahead but know how to navigate it. We have emerged from our collaboration with a dance that flows between us as we refined the message of the book, enhance and clarify the process. She is a wonderful friend and a great gift.

Cathy Davis is an artist. What a wonderful gift to hear an idea, merge with its creator, and design a look (in this case a book cover) that projects just the right message. Yes, most certainly, genius at work.

Most of all I acknowledge the thousands of folks who have encouraged me to share my Light. They have taught me that the world is ready for deeper knowledge. They are of generous spirit as you will see many examples of their lives and dreams in this book. I also acknowledge the people who are seeking this knowledge. It is time for a better world and those that turn within to discover the truth of their being will be the ones that bring it on. It is my hope that within the pages of this book, they will find themselves, heal old wounds, and become light beacons to many others.

Table of Contents

Foreword – Why this book?..1

Chapter 1
Introduction and Some History 7
Dreams and Psychology..8

Chapter 2
So, What Are Dreams? 10
Unconscious Mind and Buried Trauma..12
Subconscious Mind – Our Mental Storehouse..14
Superconscious Mind – Our Divinity at Work..15
The Astral Body..16
Awareness and Higher Consciousness...17
Illustration of the Whole Mind..18
Synopsis...19

Chapter 3
The Computer Brain 20
Brain Pathways – Habits – Compulsive Behavior.....................................22
Synopsis...23

Chapter 4
Types of Dreams...24
Synopsis...28

Chapter 5
How to Remember Your Dreams..29
Synopsis...32

Chapter 6
How to Interpret Your Dreams...33
Two Rules About Dreams..35
Synopsis...37

Chapter 7

Symbols Are Quick References 38
Universal Symbols 39
Dream Symbols and Their Meanings 43
List Your Personal Symbols Here 50
Archetypal Patterns Are Also Symbols 52
Synopsis 56

Chapter 8

Four-Step Formula for Easy Interpretation 57
Interpretation in Action—Making It Work 58
Synopsis 73

Chapter 9

Putting It All Together 74
Synopsis 76

Chapter 10

Your Life as a Dream—Tools and Exercises 77
Closed Eye Experiment 79
Making It Real—More Tools and Exercises 86
Exercise II Becoming Objective 90
Exercise III: Family as Reflection 94
Exercise IV: Present Day Life 95
Synopsis 99

Chapter 11

Holy Books Written in Symbolic Language 100
The Bible 100
Reading the Symbols—The Birth of Jesus 102
Synopsis 106

Chapter 12

The Symbolism of the Bhagavad Gita 107
Synopsis 110

Chapter 13
Lucid Dreaming – What It Is and How to Do It 111
Synopsis 113

Chapter 14
Conclusion – Where Do You Go from Here? 114

Dream Worksheets
Capture Your Dreams Here 116

About Jean Walters 124
Check out Jean's resources: 125
Other Books Written by Jean Walters 126

Foreword – Why this book?

Earth life is made of symbols. Buckminster Fuller stated, "The Universe is speaking to us all the time. We must learn to listen." Most people don't listen or pay attention, yet the messages keep coming.

Fuller was aware that life is filled with and even made up of symbols that exemplify where we, as individuals, are in our evolution. For instance, as you observe your life, you will note where you are in your personal progression. Is your life displaying joy or fear? Conflict or harmony? Are there messes that need to be cleaned up? Conflicts that need resolution? Your life reflects your thinking, beliefs, and progression. The good news is that by paying attention, you can make changes and direct your experience in ways that enrich you mentally, emotionally, physically, and spiritually.

Is your body demonstrating health or adversity? What needs balancing? The body is nothing more than a symbol of what is going on in the mind. Are you depleted or do you have stamina? The condition of your body can be traced back to the quality of thoughts gracing your mind at any time. If your thinking is confused, stressed, or overwhelmed, your body will reflect it. Contrarily, if your thoughts are peaceful, loving, open, and positive, your body demonstrates those qualities and patterns.

To take this further, look at the world. What symbols are being reflected or presented to you? Nature is always in harmony, even when it is in a state of re-balancing. For example, after a storm or tornado, nature quietly rebuilds, flows, and moves in rhythm, reconstructing whatever has been torn apart.

It is much the same with the physical body. The intelligence of the body is ever attempting to re-balance, even when we treat it badly, like the resultant hangover from a night of pouring toxins into it. Or the *cold* that follows a period of being overworked and overwhelmed. These are the body's attempt to adjust chemically and structurally. Pay attention and your body will speak to you of its needs.

Once, I was feeling poorly and I kept having a desire for pickles. This was odd because I am not much of a pickle eater. Finally, the idea of pickles seemed to scream at me. I couldn't put it off any longer. I went out and bought a jar of dill pickles and promptly ate one. Within minutes, my body felt better. The heavy, groggy, clogged feeling and lack of energy dissipated.

Later, when I mentioned the incident to my chiropractor he asked, "What about the pickle did you want?"

Me: "The vinegar."

Him: "You wanted the vinegar because your liver needed to detox. As soon as you ate the pickle, your liver released toxins in much the same way as you squeeze a lemon to release lemon juice."

How about that? The body's intelligence was sending a message that I needed to detox. I listened, followed the lead, and recovered quickly. Your body does the same thing. It will tell you what to eat and what to avoid, but you have to pay attention and follow the messages.

The same law is true of the earth. Nature continues to function. Birds know when to make nests and lay eggs, and when to fly south. Flowers bloom and trees sprout leaves at the perfect time. When cold weather comes, trees naturally go into dormancy and rest ready to prepare for the next season of sprouting forth in magnificence and color.

Yes, there are patterns and symbols we can learn from. As we understand the language of symbolism, we connect to a deeper mystery. We ultimately learn to listen to the deep wisdom of intuition or the heart. (There are many practices to help develop intuition in my book: *The Power of Knowing: 8 Step Guide to Open the Intuitive Channel and Live in Highest Consciousness.*)

Dreams are readily available and rich in this symbolic language. They teach us the workings of consciousness. Are your dreams chaotic or peaceful? Celebratory or desultory? As you tune in, are you guided to a higher reality or a course correction? I will share these kinds of dreams as we move along in discovering the various ways that symbolic language instructs us.

One of my most dramatic dreams as a teenager was very eye-opening and instructive. In it, my mother was climbing the stairs to my bedroom with an ax with the intention of ax-murdering me. Whew! At the time, my mom and I were NOT getting along and I was coming back at her whenever she tried to criticize or control me. (I am sure that hormones played into my violent reaction, as well.) Nevertheless, when I had this dream, I knew it was time to back off and that is what I did. I stopped triggering my mother. I let her have her opinion without reacting to it. I knew I was being told through my dream that I had crossed a line in my aggression. I knew that I was responsible for my own anger, and it had to stop immediately. And it did.

Now, to be clear, my mother would never have ax-murdered me or murdered me in any other way. The dream was speaking to the powerful and dramatic energy I was feeling and creating. It was clear that I had to cease and desist. Perhaps you have had a similar dream.

Holy books are filled with symbols. If you want to understand the deeper meaning of life, read the parables of Jesus in their extravagant symbolic form, like weeds removed, water into wine, and the talents, and you will be granted much wisdom. The Eastern holy book, the Bhagavad Gita, is purely symbolic and rich with instruction and wisdom.

This book, *The Magic and Mystery of Dreams,* provides insight to the language of symbols, how they appear as a dialogue from your higher mind to your conscious self, and how to use this information to hone a better life. Learn the language and you will be granted a higher perspective, one that will take you as the crow flies to a richer life.

Your conscious mind makes up stories and is often delusional in creating conflict where none exists. Your Higher Mind plays no such games and can cut to the quick with no-nonsense information. In other words, dreams and symbolic language are honest and forthright, never critical or negative. They simply state the truth with a no-nonsense approach.

Where there is imbalance, there is also balance. The saying is: *The solution to the problem is in the problem.* In other words, the problem holds the solution. Look to the symbolic references and you will find the way to the solution and the balance.

In this book, I approach symbolism from different vantage points: the magic and mystery of daydreams and night dreams, the symbolism offered in holy books like the Bible and Bhagavad Gita, and the symbols that show up in your daily earth experience. For instance, every person in your life (harmonious and inharmonious) reflects *you* in some way. Crabby Aunt Mildred illustrates a crabby aspect of you. When you no longer react to her negativity or take her criticism personally, you will have transcended that aspect and won't be bothered by her. She essentially disappears, no longer an important symbol for you. The same is true of your angelic friend who always shows up to help. She is you also. This angel friend symbolizes your kind, helpful qualities. Look at who you admire. These folks are also symbols. More on that later.

Weather conditions. Yes, pay attention to your reaction to weather conditions.

Here is an example: A couple was on their way to my class when they observed the dark funnel cloud of a tornado crossing the road in front of them. They could see it, but it did not interfere with their travel. When they arrived at class, they were excited to explore its meaning.

I asked them what in their life was illustrating the destructiveness of a tornado. The answer immediately came: the fellow's mother. By recognizing her negative energy, they knew what had to be done to defuse it. Watching the funnel cloud helped to clarify the situation for them. Note that the tornado did not touch them, and the "parent" could not touch them with her negativity either. They were at all times safe and they knew it.

So, by paying attention to symbols, things that may have gone unnoticed before, become relevant. Who or what triggers you and in what way? Your reactions inform you of your emotional, psychological wounds, and your desires, lessons, and archetypal patterns. Paying attention can evoke healing. Positive reactions inform you as to what inspires you.

We all demonstrate archetypal patterns, such as the warrior or victim. They illustrate the path we are destined to take in life. By understanding these patterns, we can work with them and reveal their highest potential. This is how we cooperate with our internal or higher (spiritual) plan.

It does not mean, as a *warrior*, you have to join the military and go into battle. It can mean that, as a *warrior*, you are to stand tall in conflict and not relinquish until you have achieved your end goal. Think of a civil-rights or political activist, or someone geared to transform healthcare, childcare, or the financial system. These people have warrior archetypes and they use them to foster change in the system.

Everyone has a *victim* archetypal pattern and can learn to rise above it and avoid a life of self-pity. The *victim* archetype is a symbol of the world we live in, meaning we tend to focus on victims. As yet, the world in general has not recognized the immense power of change at hand. As victims, we tend to react to situations rather than consciously, purposefully pursuing and installing change.

To master victim-consciousness, we must take responsibility for our choices and our lives (with no excuses) and be willing to adjust and transform to things as they move purposefully toward a higher vision.

The study of symbols is rich with wisdom. In this book, I give you a proprietary Four-Step Formula to help make the dream you are living in easier to understand. It applies to every day and night dream and situation. As you master the formula, it will give you a shortcut to higher understanding and appreciation of the situations you have created and, potentially, ways to move through them.

If you are willing to accept responsibility for your life, grasping the meaning of symbols will provide a way through the maze of your experiences. Your journey of growth will become easier, simpler, and more profound.

Chapter 1

Introduction and Some History

Dreams have been a source of inspiration and mystery for hundreds of years. The end of the world has been predicted from dreams many times. These dreams illustrated the end of something in the dreamer's world: a situation, relationship, career, etc. Dreams have also served as subjects of entertainment and fright. They have played a part in many cultures and folklore.

Throughout history, dreams have illustrated man's evolution. Ancient and present-day cultures, such as the Hopi Indians, Peruvian Shamans, and Egyptians, derived deep meaning from dreams and visions and used them for guidance.

Many holy books speak of dreams. The Bible, for instance, refers to dreams often. One of the most famous references is about Joseph, son of Abraham, who wore the coat of many colors. Joseph was rejected by his brothers and sold into slavery, yet he became a valued advisor to the Egyptian ruler because he was able to interpret the ruler's dreams. Through his ability to understand dreams, Joseph helped the Pharaoh set policy and saved the country from severe years of famine.

Warnings have also come through dreams. In the Christ story, Joseph, husband of Mary and father of Jesus, was instructed in a dream to take his family and leave Nazareth to avoid the evil intentions of King Herod.

The Book of Revelations in the New Testament is comprised entirely of the dreams of John while exiled on the Isle of Patmos. These dreams are considered futuristic.

Likewise, it is with you. Your dreams offer insight that can change the course of your life. Instead of living life on the surface, you have access to the unprejudiced, non-judgmental soul view of your experiences and activities. You will know when it is time to change tracks. It will be clear when you have violated an important value or when it is time to up your game. The subconscious never lies and everything is portrayed in your dreams.

If you are lost in your dream, identify how you are lost in your life. The cues are there. The need is to identify them. If you are following the guidance in your dreams, it will be indicated. Dreams never lie. They emanate from your own consciousness. They present the truth of your circumstances and your reactions in clear, bold colors and identifiable symbols.

Dreams and Psychology

Over the years, the field of psychology has developed many theories and techniques regarding dreams. Many are used in psychotherapy. Sigmund Freud, the man considered the Father of Psychoanalysis, was one of the most famous proponents of dreams. He proposed one of the first theories concerning dream analysis. His idea was that dreams reveal suppressed desires and forbidden sexual urges. (That might be saying something about Freud.)

Carl Jung differed with Freud's assessment. Jung developed his own ideas about dreams as coming from what he termed "the collective unconscious" and representing man's desire to create. Jung saw dreams as an important tool in therapy.

In psychotherapy, many consider Jung's efforts at interpreting symbols as laying the foundation for all future dream work. Contrarily, Alfred Adler, psychotherapist, interpreted dreams as an expression of man's desire for power and security.

A more current theory on dream analysis is offered in Gestalt therapy. Here it is suggested that dreams provide a means for self-integration. This theory poses that all persons, objects, and features in the dream are parts of the dreamer's personality, the point being to interpret each item as relative to the dreamer.

Metaphysicians, those who study the Universe as a cosmology with organized laws and progressions, interpret dreams in much the same way. Their theory is that dreams are a running commentary from the self about the self. When they are viewed objectively as a statement, or even as a critique of the dreamer's previous day's activities and reactions to same, they hold a wealth of self-knowledge. The assertion is that when dreams are properly understood, they offer an accurate resource to be used for personal and spiritual growth. The beauty of dreams is that this resource and information is available to anyone disciplined enough to learn the symbolic language of dreams and tap into their messages.

In my experience, information obtained in dreams has been instrumental, even profound, in helping me make decisions, navigate life, and manage a variety of life changes. The same is true for many clients who have sought understanding of their dream messages. The information has proven beneficial in understanding health conditions, relationships, career challenges, and opportunities.

This book offers a simplified methodology of interpretation and a universally recognized list of symbols that can be used, learned, and developed for use in dream interpretation and appreciating life. Plus, there is guidance in applying this information to clarify your experiences as seen with my fore-mentioned dream.

With on-going use over time, you will be able to comprehend the patterns and challenges of life and make appropriate adjustments to move forward. It will also change the way you view earth life, as there is much to learn by examining the symbols that show up day by day. We are all in constant communication with the Universe.

Chapter 2

So, What Are Dreams?

According to the Merriam-Webster Dictionary, *Dreams are a series of thought images or emotions occurring during sleep or in day-dreams or reverie; something notable for its beauty, excellence and enjoyable quality.* This definition states what dreams are, but not how or why they occur, or even what to do with them once you have one.

Dreams are the way we process our life experiences. This is how it works: dreaming occurs when attention is withdrawn from the five physical senses: sight, taste, smell, hearing, and touch. This withdrawal happens most often while asleep, but it may also be experienced while awake. Awake dreams are called daydreams, visions, or reveries. Whether awake or asleep, the same process is involved: attention is removed from the physical senses and focus is placed on the inner world.

It follows that there must be a part of the mind that is only accessible when one's attention is withdrawn from the external world. The part of the mind activated at these times is the subconscious mind. Let's explore the various parts of the mind and how they impact personal awareness.

The mind is composed of three parts, or levels or vibrational energies: conscious, subconscious, and Superconscious. The part of the mind we are most familiar with is the conscious mind because we use it while awake. The conscious mind works in direct contact with the brain. It is attentive as we move through daily activities. It is also considered the reasoning or analytical mind and the mind of the ego. When we are inundated with mental chatter, the egoic mind is running the show.

Indulging mental chatter is a block to achieving personal space, silence, and calmness. It poses a block to self-awareness.

In the beginning, you were born with a blank slate (conscious mind); blank in that there was no personal information recorded or stored in the brain. Thus, your primary brain function was to run the autonomic systems: breathing, digesting, eliminating, cell division, etc.

When you cried for the first time, you began to experience earth life. This information, as well as the resultant response, was recorded in the conscious and subconscious minds and imprinted within your brain like a personal computer. Each day, you added information as new awareness was calculated. The brain is very much like a computer, storing information as it is available. This is not to say that the brain is the conscious mind, for it is not. The brain is only a tool for the mind to use. It is a conduit. The mind is much vaster than the brain.

Until you begin to experience and record information, you are only functioning with the subconscious mind. A child functions primarily from the subconscious mind for the first seven years of life. It is the reason the child knows things that were not taught in his short experience, like how to operate a musical instrument, why people behave as they do, who to trust, and how to be creative. By around the age of seven, the conscious mind has accumulated enough information to direct activities and make decisions. In other words, the child now knows the family dynamics and what is expected.

The more information (experience) that is recorded, the more dominant the conscious mind becomes, diminishing conscious contact with the subconscious. The experience is similar to a patio glass door being opened. In the beginning, the patio door is completely closed and allows only subconscious awareness to shine through. As the individual is indoctrinated, the door begins to open with awareness of systems and beliefs that are required and expected. Children readily give in to this indoctrination because it appears that to be part of a family group, agreement is required. Survival requires that the child subjugate to the family dynamic.

All voluntary action is directed by the conscious mind, which is the mind we use to observe, reason, learn, express, draw conclusions, and accumulate knowledge. When the conscious mind is quieted, as in sleep or hypnosis, the subconscious mind comes forward. As it does, vast information is available that may not easily be accessed during the waking state.

The subconscious mind represents a more subtle vibratory energy that lies beneath the chatter of the conscious mind. It is essentially subjugated by the conscious mind's attention in the material world. We become aware of its presence only when the conscious mind has been quieted. Hence, we may experience the subconscious mind when our reasoning faculty is lulled to passivity while we dream, have intuitive flashes, experience deep concentration, meditate, or undergo hypnosis.

Getting in touch with the subconscious mind might again be compared to closing a sliding patio door. When the conscious and subconscious minds overlap one another, as when the patio doors are open, there is a lot of interference (blockage) to the clear, objective awareness of the subconscious mind pouring through into individual awareness. But when the conscious mind is pushed aside (patio doors closed) as in sleep, the subconscious mind is able to operate to its fullest, thus letting inner knowledge and awareness shine through unimpeded.

Often, one will experience a similar state of mind as the patio doors being closed on the subconscious awareness shining through, This occurs when driving a car for long periods of time. The condition is called *road hypnosis*. The driver of a car becomes hypnotized by the monotony of watching the road pass by. The conscious mind becomes so bored, it moves aside and the subconscious mind is able to operate without impediment. This is when problems are solved, answers to questions show up, projects are completed, etc. The driver might experience a dream-like state of images. When the driver *wakes up* and takes conscious control of the vehicle, the subconscious state of hypnosis is ended.

Unconscious Mind and Buried Trauma

There is a segment of the conscious mind called the unconscious. This stores seemingly forgotten or hidden information such as guilt, shame, fear, prejudice, unfulfilled desire, hopes, dreams, and aspirations. This is to say that, although you may not be aware of your fears or desires, they exist and can be triggered by a situation and come forward into awareness. The unconscious has been formed throughout your lifetime and because you have this pool of accumulated (often misunderstood or misinterpreted) experience, you will tend to react compulsively and unconsciously to situations based on ideas fed into and stored there.

For example, if you were bitten by a dog when you were a child and felt terror, you would have stored the memory in the unconscious mind. When confronted by a dog in the present time, the fear again arises. In the immediate situation, the dog may be docile and gentle. You may reason it is irrational to be afraid of it. Yet, if the memory of terror had not been consciously worked through and understood, there will be ongoing irrational reactions to dogs due to the negative past association. Understand that all fears can be examined from a more objective, calm perspective. The person can be freed from continued negative reactions in the future.

If these irrational fears are not cleared, it is understandable that people negatively react to bad driving, slippery roads, rudeness, altercations, anything that can be interpreted through a misunderstood past experience. Hence, abusive relationships, bad behavior, and road rage are the result.

Using the story of the memory of the dog bite, it is easy to see why a person develops all kinds of illogical ideas and stresses. Most ideas are based on beliefs that have been presented during a high emotional outpouring. This could mean being upbraided in front of friends as a child and unconsciously storing a deep sense of humiliation and insecurity. Or, perhaps almost losing a loved one or being involved in an accident provoked an uncontrolled fear state. Perhaps a person decides he was at fault and carries that guilt around forever. These are the types of beliefs and memories stored in the unconscious and show up in dreams. Why? Because they have never been resolved and they need to be.

Is there a memory of being trapped by a ranting emotionally charged adult? An intense delivery of righteousness, indignation, fear, or rage can throw a child into a hypnotic state. Perhaps the rant was on the value of honesty or the inappropriateness of lying or stealing, etc. Because the diatribe was delivered loudly and with extreme emotional thrust, it was dramatically recorded in the child's consciousness. The child may have felt guilty or traumatized. Henceforth, when that grown child fudges on the truth, tells a lie, or steals credit, there is an inward reaction with similar emotions: guilt, shame, rage. The recorded "rant" may even go off in the person's mind and reminds him to feel bad.

Until this memory is processed, reasoned through, and understood, the tendency will be to compulsively react when someone raises his voice, when the subject of honesty comes up, or when an authority figure begins an emotional tirade. These unfiltered memories will also show up in a dream state. Why? Because buried memories are brought up to illustrate the wounds or psychological state of the dreamer and how that individual has erringly interpreted events (past or present). In other words, if it is real in one's mind, it is real.

Subconscious Mind – Our Mental Storehouse

Let's move on to the subconscious mind, which is the mind behind or underneath the conscious mind. Its essence is finer and subtler than the thinking, reasoning quality of the conscious mind. You might say that these minds are layered and vibrate at slightly different frequencies.

Because we function primarily from the subconscious (the feeling or intuitive mind), during the first seven years of life, young children are naturally imaginative, instinctive, and psychic. For example, they know when people are lying or untrustworthy. There is a saying that you cannot fool children or animals. That's because children and animals do not understand words. Therefore, they are not fooled by them. They sense each situation and person and react accordingly. Since their rational faculty is undeveloped, they follow an inner sensory facility rather than analyze or reason their circumstances.

Each one of us brings the subconscious depository of experiences and understandings (the soul) with us from incarnation to incarnation. All previously learned lessons, understandings, talents, and expressions are a permanent part of the subconscious mind. It is like a bank value of experience and knowing.

All consciously understood experiences become a permanent part of the subconscious mind. For example, if in one lifetime you develop a brilliant ability with mathematics and made practical use of this talent, you will carry over this knack to progressive lifetimes. You can see from this example why individuals have natural abilities, such as composing music, playing musical instruments, sewing, construction, or intuitive skills, etc. These have been accrued in other lifetimes and carried through to the present. Thus, the subconscious mind serves as a storehouse for past knowledge and wisdom and memories of experiences gleaned in the present lifetime.

If you want to remember a childhood experience, you draw this memory from the storehouse of the subconscious. Beliefs, ideas, and behaviors you were taught and experiences you have had in your current lifetime are ever available. They often direct your present involvements from an involuntary point of view. For instance, if you had been taught to believe that you must work hard to make money, and this admonition had been repeated and perhaps stated with very definite stern emotion, then no doubt, your sensitive, child-like psyche had been impressed and the belief has become your own. This is true even though you may have observed others performing easy tasks and earning large amounts of money.

The subconscious mind helps to guide your current experience by out-picturing your beliefs into material reality. This particular condition of limitation will not change until you choose to review the mental construct and determine it to be incorrect, irrational, and unrealistic.

Through careful reprogramming and working out a disciplined new scenario, you will cause the old view to give way to a new one, such as *money flows naturally into my life. By using my natural abilities, I will always have plenty of money.*

The opportunity exists for you to live life any way you want. But primarily, you are controlled by unconscious beliefs that you act out day after day. You have to deliberately rethink your original premise or reinterpret an experience to draw a new conclusion. Dreams will expose these old beliefs making it readily apparent what needs to change.

The subconscious also works with the brain in an involuntary way. That is to say that when you are not directing your breathing, bodily processes, and experiences consciously, the subconscious mind takes over and does it for you. Your body knows how to digest food, take in oxygen, process nutrients, make new blood cells, and eliminate waste, to name a few automatic functions.

Superconscious Mind – Our Divinity at Work

The Superconscious Mind is the highest resonant or deepest part of the mind. It is the spark or life-force from the Creator. It is also referred to as the High Self or Divine Mind. In the Bible, it is referred to as the Lord God or I Am. This is the Light within that is acknowledged as the ruler of one's inner Kingdom.

Each part of the mind has its own energy and substance. The energy of the Superconscious Mind vibrates at the highest frequency and is only perceivable with the fine-tuning that occurs in meditation.

Each part of the mind slows its vibration as it projects outward to the physical world. In other words, the lower the mind, the slower the vibration, or the higher the mind, the faster the vibration and finer the substance. This expression of energy proceeds outward to the dense plane where the vibration of matter is so slow as to be perceivable with the dull mechanisms of the physical eyes. This heavy, gross movement we term the material world. This is the place we learn our lessons. It is our cosmic schoolroom.

The mind has many levels and densities. It is like an iceberg in the arctic. That tiny peak of the iceberg showing above the surface of the water only hints at a massive structure beneath the waterline that is much greater and more substantial. In the same way, what we see of man with our physical eyes hints at a much greater structure lying beneath the surface or out of sight of the physical senses. We are each a multi-faceted, feeling, sensing, creative being. When we are able to tap into these deeper reaches of mind, our knowledge, awareness, and power will be unlimited. Sometimes we get glimpses of this potential in meditation or dreams.

The Astral Body

Just as one uses different types of vehicles when traveling by land, air, or water, so too, each part of the mind uses a different vehicle to experience. For example, astral projection (an out-of-body experience) is accomplished by focusing attention in the subconscious or feeling mind. The astral body is an inner body, much more subtle than the material body. It is as real to the subconscious mind as the physical body is to the conscious mind. They exist simultaneously. The physical body and conscious mind rest during sleep. While dreaming, the astral body and subconscious mind become active. In dreams, the astral body may be illustrated by flying.

Together, the conscious, subconscious, and Superconscious make up the whole mind. The conscious mind reasons, analyzes, identifies, and focuses on the material world and interprets conscious experiences. The subconscious mind works to fulfill the desires, thoughts, and experiences of the conscious mind. It serves as a storehouse of information, knowledge, and wisdom. The Superconscious Mind, as the higher mind, sustains the creative plan and purpose for existence.

Awareness and Higher Consciousness

Conscious awareness of your highest mind can be achieved by harmonizing the conscious and subconscious levels to the finer frequency of the Superconscious. This is achieved through discipline, meaning the conscious mind must become still. Stillness allows alignment. Think of sitting at the beach and quieting your mind so that you are completely present in the stillness and vastness of the sky and the ocean. In this deep stillness, you connect with your most profound Self, the Light of the soul. As you learn to function in deep stillness, the purpose of earth life can be known and fulfilled.

When the light of love can radiate and express without inhibition through each level of mind, we can perfect our status as reflecting our Divine imprint or archetype. This is when we become an unconditional vehicle of Love and Light.

As we learn through each experience, we progressively drop egoic values, smallness, materialist necessities, and beliefs that we were trained to accept. That is when we let go of fear, shame, guilt, and shallowness so that we might aspire to a higher ideal and move to a consciousness of freedom, love, and joy.

In dreams, parents are an illustration of the Superconscious Mind. The reason for this is that, as children, we looked up to our parents and considered them to know everything. They were like Gods to us. So, whether or not our parents fulfilled their "God-like" roles, in dreams, they still represent the Higher Self. Other symbols that relate to the Superconscious Mind would be anyone we consider evolved. This might be a favorite teacher, a religious figure, or an exalted master. This symbol will differ from person to person.

Illustration of the Whole Mind

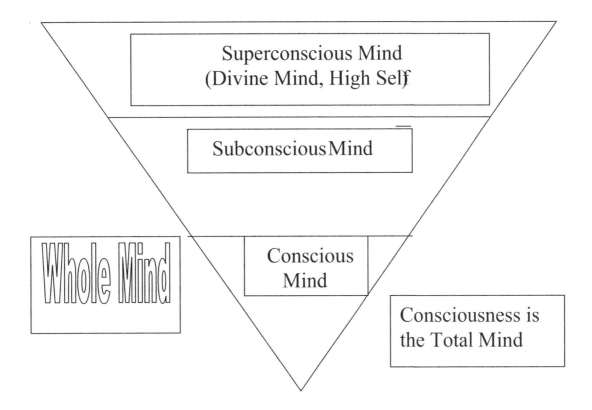

Superconscious Mind (High Self/Divine Mind): This mind vibrates at the highest frequency. This fine energy is at the core of your existence. Its substance is so subtle it cannot be detected by man-made instruments. It is the Light within, the God-Self, Divine Being, High Self, I Am. It holds within the purpose for existence.

Subconscious Mind: This mind is the storehouse for information, the Soul of man. It contains the fine substance we use to manifest our desires and fears. *That which you focus on, you experience.* It lies behind and layered within the conscious mind.

Conscious Mind: This is the mind we use and experience while awake. It reasons and analyzes. It comprises our conscious identity and often is referred to as the mind of the ego or the "chatter mind." There are two parts to the conscious mind: the conscious and the unconscious. The unconscious stores unresolved issues such as guilt, fear, unfulfilled desires, hopes, and misunderstandings. The vibrational frequency is the slowest of the three elements of mind.

Synopsis

- Dreams are important sources of objective, non-judgmental information and wisdom from your higher mind.
- Dreaming occurs when attention is withdrawn from the five physical senses. This can happen in sleep or an awakened state, such as daydreams, reveries, and visions.
- The mind is composed of three elements: conscious, subconscious, and Superconscious. Each part has a role and purpose to play in the grand scheme of the evolution of consciousness.
- The unconscious mind is part of the conscious mind. It stores hidden, buried, and programmed ideas that have created conflict for the dreamer. The unconscious also holds unresolved feelings such as guilt, prejudice, fear, shame, and unfulfilled desires. These *memories* are often triggered by everyday events and, therefore, show up in dreams. This gives the dreamer an opportunity to face these issues.
- All experiences and understandings are recorded in the subconscious mind. The feeling quality comes forward as the dreamer's psyche determines the necessity. The point of all memory and experience is to evolve and grow, to become free, expressive, and unconditionally loving beings.
- The brain is man's computer for storing information relating to the present lifetime.
- The subconscious mind can be accessed in dreams, hypnosis, or meditation. It can offer valuable insight that can be used to process experiences and learn lessons.
- Awareness of the Superconscious Mind is achieved as we subjugate the conscious mind to the desires and values of the higher mind. Letting go of illusions, false ideas, and negative emotions and interpretations allows space for Truth and Light to enter the mind. The mind then becomes a vehicle for love.

Chapter 3

The Computer Brain

The brain is man's computer. It is a sophisticated mechanism that selectively records experiences and then compares these to information previously filed. This data is accumulated from the time of birth and is obtainable when triggered by a new experience that has the same quality of energy or vibration as the previously filed information.

Being similar to a computer, the brain cannot give you information that has not been previously recorded. For instance, if you have never been ice-skiing, it would be hard to relate or describe the joy or freedom of movement on the ice to another person. If you have never eaten an artichoke, how would you relate the taste and texture?

The subconscious or feeling portion of the brain is accessed through the thalamus (chamber). The thalamus plays an important part in the dreaming process. All sensations are first registered in the subconscious and then later in the conscious mind. This is why children and animals function instinctively. They are using the old brain or animal brain (feeling only) and have not developed the hardware or programmed grey matter of the mature human.

Every sensation that comes to us through any or all of the senses is mediated first through the thalamus, is next invested with a feeling value in these upper reaches of the brain, then is passed on to various portions of the brain that requires the information for proper action. Example: Your finger touches a hot stove. Through the sense of touch, nerves register a response and send a message to the brain. The message enters the subconscious, where it is interpreted and action is determined. A nerve response is transmitted to remove the finger from the stove. Feeling is registered first, followed by reasoning within the conscious mind.

Every sensation that comes to us creates either a negative or a positive feeling, depending on the way it is interpreted in the upper brain. This can be called pleasant or unpleasant. All words, actions, and deeds (from self and others) create either a positive (pleasant) or negative (unpleasant) feeling in us.

To illustrate this point, words creating negative reactions are pain, fear, guilt, debt, hate. Words giving birth to positive reactions might be love, happiness, peace, contentment, appreciation. Visual images evoking positive effects are smiles and laughter. Those that cause negative effects are frowns, slamming doors, arguing.

There is a constant interplay between the thinking portion of the brain and the feeling part of the brain. The memories associated with past experiences recreate the same feeling when a similar experience occurs. This can be a conscious or unconscious reaction and a negative or positive response. It is interesting to note that, because of this programming set into the brain, people emotionally react by buying things, joining clubs, drinking alcohol, establishing relationships, making an investment, or getting into fights based on emotional impulse rather than considering a rational approach to the situation.

For instance, if you have had a difficult day at work—perhaps lost a good client or invested money badly—you might react by stopping for a drink, getting a speeding ticket, or starting an unwarranted argument. At this point, it might be said that you have lost your reasoning capability and are reacting purely from emotion. Instead of chalking up a tough day to "It can happen," and letting it go, you succumb to a mental program and expectation that *you must always succeed and no failure is acceptable.* You fall into emotional distress and let it take over, steering into more conflict. Generally, these types of events come into being because people are unrealistic and downright mean to themselves. Of course, this experience will show up in dreams as chaos, guns going off, crashes, or other images of helplessness and being out of control.

In the dream state, the brain interprets impressions from the subconscious mind in images that the dreamer is familiar with. As pictures, symbols, and feelings in dreams are presented, clues are offered to reveal the state of the dreamer's spiritual, emotional, mental, and physical condition, as well as where the individual is as far as personal growth is involved. The dreamer has the opportunity to put these clues to work and progress in addressing emotional reactivity and unresolved issues.

Following this reasoning, nightmares would reveal the dreamer's fears while happy dreams would reflect a pleasant or peaceful state of being. The subconscious mind objectively draws on the dreamer's waking thoughts, ideas, feelings, and actions and reflects these back in the dream state.

Brain Pathways – Habits – Compulsive Behavior

One more thing about the brain. Things that are repeated as habits (habit patterns) such as brushing your teeth daily, calling your mother every Sunday, getting angry while driving in traffic, or playing tennis on Tuesday, construct pathways in the brain. That is why you can turn on the car engine and drive to work without thinking about how to get there. You relinquish control to the subconscious mind. It takes over and drives you right to work.

Habit patterns or brain pathways can also form from feeling guilty when you felt you took advantage of someone, or if you crumble when you have to speak before a group, or if you are afraid during a thunderstorm.

Your dreams will exemplify these brain pathways by illustrating someone or something that operates compulsively, for that is what a habit is: compulsive behavior. It might show up as the symbol of a rabbit running and hiding when in danger, or a wounded animal hiding under the bed for self-protection. The animal is acting compulsively out of fear. This symbol would illustrate the dreamer's compulsiveness.

Synopsis

- The brain, a sophisticated mechanism, selectively records experiences and accumulates data from the time of birth. This information is triggered and brought forward by new experiences with the same quality as the old ones.
- The brain feeds back only that which has been experienced or imagined.
- Everything seen, heard, and felt, past and present, is associated and vested with a feeling value, then plays out in life.
- Sensations are interpreted in the upper (or old/animal) brain according to pleasant or unpleasant feeling values.
- People act on impulse according to the type of programming set in the brain.
- In the dream state, images and symbols are presented with the same emotional quality as when awake. This objective presentation in dreams serves as a clue for the dreamer to resolve issues and process lessons.
- Compulsive behavior, such as habits, which are brain pathways, is often illustrated in dreams as compulsive people or animals. Animals act out of compulsion instinctively because they don't analyze or reason.

Chapter 4

Types of Dreams

Dreams fall into several categories. By far, the most prevalent dream category is a portrayal of your state of consciousness regarding yourself and the events in your life. This is arrived at by simply processing the previous days' experiences. These dreams offer insight as to what is working and what is not, what fears are prevalent in your consciousness and how joy is promoted.

Each night as you sleep, the subconscious mind processes your experiences of the previous days. What turns up in a dream is a direct, objective view of how you are experiencing life. It reveals your prevalent theme, how you actually feel about it, what has you befuddled, why you are experiencing it, and gives hints on what to do next. This straightforward, objective view provides clarity and offers the opportunity to make improvements.

This attitudinal information in dreams gives you a direct approach to growth. Unconscious fears and reactions become obvious. The opportunity to make adjustments becomes clear. The process is illuminating and transformative.

Another category of dreams includes what I term *health dreams*. In health dreams, the subconscious mind is calling attention to the condition of the physical body and/or the mental-emotional state of the dreamer as it relates to wellbeing.

For example, this verbal statement was presented in a dream: "Your body is like a garbage can." In this simple, straightforward dream, the dreamer got to examine what she puts into her body that is making it *like a garbage can*. (Hint: lots of junk food.)

Another health dream illustrated a boiler that was red hot and about to blow. The red-hot boiler was the dreamer. The dream clearly illustrated the rage that was brewing inside the dreamer and it was about to blow, indicating danger, either to himself or another.

Precognitive dreams create another category of dream types. The subconscious mind does not have the time-space constraints relative to the conscious mind and linear time. It has the potential to peek ahead and view tomorrow's happenings. While the dreamer sleeps, it reports its findings. Usually, precognitive dreams have a different quality of energy expression. With practice, the dreamer will learn to identify this subtle variation. In actuality, the number of precognitive dreams one may experience is small by comparison to the first type of dreams: the state of consciousness dream, which can be seen as a clear report of where you stand attitudinally in your life.

One of the symbols I have noticed with precognitive dreams is the presence of mud. Mud is more fluid than packed stable earth. That is why I believe it is used in this type of dream. Future happenings are not yet set in solid material form, so the mud presents a state of becoming, yet not yet manifest. It is like clay in the process of being molded. With this one exception, the symbols in precognitive dreams are the same as all other dreams.

Another dream type is the dreamer's *quest for information*. These dreams offer "answers." In other words, dreams are a great way to request information and get answers to current challenges. Often when awake, the mind is continuously occupied with mental chatter and various requirements of living. Answers don't come through. When the mind is stilled in sleep, these answers will surface in a dream.

The subconscious mind, being connected to every level of mind, has availability to infinite stores of wisdom. Therefore, the potential to access assistance in dreams is endless. If the dreamer is open and willing, the mind will plumb the depths of this supply and bring forth new ideas, suggestions, inspirations, or answers. When the request or need is clear, the subconscious happily obliges. That is to say, when you go to sleep with a thought or question weighing on your mind, or you are consciously asking for help, your inner mind offers solutions in your dream.

The scientist-inventor, Thomas Edison, used this method often. When it appeared he was stuck while working on a project in his laboratory, he would call on the subconscious mind and its storehouse of information.

Edison kept a cot in the laboratory for such occasions. When he found himself stymied and unable to ascertain his next step, he would take a nap. Before closing his eyes, he asked the subconscious mind for the answer to his problem. Then he went to sleep. When Edison reclined, he placed a small object in his hand. As he relaxed in sleep, his hand opened, the object dropped to the floor making a sound, and he would be aroused.

Edison had programmed his mind to awaken at the sound of the object hitting the floor. Whatever thought or image he had in his mind when he woke up, he considered to be his answer. He followed through by putting his solution to work in his experiments. Edison was a great inventor with more than 200 registered patents, No doubt, the assistance he received from the subconscious was invaluable in his work. He used this method often.

You can use this unlimited source of information also. It is a matter of programming a request for assistance into the subconscious mind before going to sleep. As you awaken, you use the information given in your dream as your answer. With time and practice, you can develop this method into a highly efficient skill, as did Thomas Edison.

Polish Nobel Prize winner Marie Curie was also the benefactor of receiving answers in dreams. She was working on a difficult formula involving radium in her laboratory and could not solve the problem. She finally let go and went home. Later that night, she woke from a dream and a formula was given to her. She quickly wrote it down and went back to bed. The next day, she recovered her written dream and discovered that the formula she had written during the night contained the answer she needed.

The last category of dreams concerns *visitations*, usually by people who have died. For instance, a friend (or parent, or sister, or child) dies and you experience a dream where that person is smiling and waving and telling you (telepathically) that he or she is fine. No need to worry. All is well.

Many, if not most people have a dream of this sort. A loved one who has passed away appears to comfort them. In these dreams, they should be taken for what they are: literally, a dream of reassurance and comfort from someone loved and is no longer in the physical realm.

One last note on types of dreams: *recurring dreams* have not been mentioned. These would fall under the first category relative to processing one's day because they provide information about the dreamer's state of mind. In much the same manner as people approach a particular situation with redundancy, these dreams are also redundant. Example: if you are always angry when your neighbor plays loud music, your dream will pick up on the redundant pattern of being angry.

Recurring dreams are redundant because the situation the dreamer is experiencing is redundant. The dream restates a message. Once the dreamer has taken appropriate action on whatever message is portrayed, the dream stops. In other words, because dreams are a commentary reflecting the dreamer's state of consciousness, by altering the situation and/or attitude, the dream becomes irrelevant. Often, fear is restated in a dream, like being chased, feeling attacked, someone trying to gain entry into your home. Another common repetitive dream is feeling lost, not knowing where you are going. These themes reflect the dreamer's state of feeling lost in life.

Synopsis

- Dreams are indicators of the attitudes, experiences, and states of mind of the dreamer's move through life. They also report health conditions, can be precognitive, and provide solutions and answers to challenges. Occasionally, dreams will reveal a visitation from someone who has passed on to other dimensions. These are primarily consoling in nature.

- Thomas Edison used dreams as a problem-solving mechanism. Marie Curie received a completed scientific formula through a dream. We can also ask for dreams to supply answers, solutions, and insight.

- Loved ones who have passed on in life (died) often show up in dreams to offer consolation and comfort to the dreamer.

- Recurring dreams represent recurring situations in life. Sometimes these are joyful and sometimes these are anxiety-provoking patterns that have not yet been resolved. When the situation triggering the dream is resolved, the dream ceases.

Chapter 5

How to Remember Your Dreams

When we dream, the conscious mind is at rest and experiences occur in the subconscious mind. The dream world can be exciting, scary, inspirational, informational, or match any feeling component possible in the awake state. They can be chock full of memorable images and lack nothing in regard to entertainment or amusement. Why then, do we have a difficult time remembering our dreams? Because we experience dreams at a different level of consciousness than our normal waking life.

As we awaken, we are actually transferring our attention to another distinctive world. This would be comparable to sleeping in Arizona and waking up in New York. As soon as we open our eyes and begin thinking about our experience in New York, we quickly forget about Arizona. As a result of the rapid loss of memory of Arizona and of the dream adventure we had there, it is important to be prepared quickly to record the dream upon awakening. A dream is like an echo in the mind. The first time we hear it, it is loud. But it rapidly fades. A dream fades and is lost altogether if not recorded when fresh in the mind.

This rapid loss can be counteracted by making a gradual transition from sleeping to waking. Lie still, eyes closed. Let the awake state come in slowly. You may relax and stay in the dream state or recall it easily as you accustom yourself to dreaming and accept the dream experience as real.

Many people experience an impressionable dream, briefly ponder its meaning upon awakening, file it away for later review, and lose it, never to be retrieved again.

Most dreamers dismiss their dream memories as trivial brain waves produced during sleep to make haphazard images. They call these images "crazy," "wild," and lacking relevance. The reason for this is simple. These people do not understand the dream language. This would be equivalent to a Frenchman conversing with you in fluid French when all you understand is English. If this dialogue were to continue, you would soon grow tired and walk away. You don't understand French. You don't know what he is saying to you and you don't care either.

It is no wonder that people say they do not remember their dreams. They are listening to the subconscious mind spout symbols that they do not comprehend and have no way of interpreting. Dreams to them are muddled, confused, irrational energy. If one were to learn French, the Frenchman could be an interesting informative companion. If dreams were to be understood, they could be a phenomenally rich resource of knowledge. The trick is to learn the language. You will find as you work with dreams that there is a distinct dream language. The more you connect feelings and symbols (more on that later), the easier the language is to understand.

Inasmuch as we have spent time ignoring and dismissing our dreams, we have established a block in recalling them. But this interference can be overcome. Essentially, we have told ourselves that dreams are meaningless and there is no point to remembering them. It is a waste of time contemplating their messages. Since this has been our thinking, it has also become the program for the brain-computer. If we understand how a computer works, we know that once we program it, it obediently follows that program until the program is deleted or changed. In other words, the brain-computer must be reprogrammed about dreams.

This is actually a simple task, but it does require consistency and discipline. Owing to this requirement, it would be good to consider how important it is to you to remember your dreams. If it is not really crucial to you, you will easily lose your discipline and soon forget. You will be back to square one.

Each night before you retire, take a few minutes to talk to your subconscious mind. You will actually be talking to yourself since the subconscious mind is really a part of you. The concept of remembering your dreams must be reiterated along with the appreciation of dreams and the gift they offer. For instance, you might affirm: *My dreams come easily to me; I remember them easily. Each night, I receive clear, impressionable dreams and awaken to write them down. I am grateful for all my dream memories. My subconscious mind wakes me at the conclusion of my dream so that I can record it. I joyfully awaken and record my dreams. I am appreciative of all my dream impressions and gratefully receive them as inspiration and awaken to record them. I am thankful for my dreams.*

When you program your mind in this way, you will be redundant. Your feeling quality must be sincere and appreciative.

Perform this discipline every night before retiring to bed. In a night or two, you will begin awakening with a dream. It is crucial to let this process unfold at its own rate. If the first night you awaken with only a feeling, a color, or one image, be sure to write this down. As your subconscious notes your dedication, the dream impressions will come more fluidly and abundantly.

It is best, at least in the beginning, to defer asking for solutions to problems, since you have not yet become sophisticated in dream language and deciphering symbols. Give yourself time and you will be able to deftly move through the dream process with clarity and knowing.

To strengthen your resolve to the subconscious mind, you must follow up with physical activity. The first action to take is to have a pen and paper by your bedside, within easy reach, so you can awaken quickly and record your dreams. This action reinforces to the subconscious mind that you mean busines. It will subsequently manifest your desires by presenting a dream and urging you to awaken.

There is no point to ask for dreams while lacking sufficient discipline to record them. Your subconscious mind will not be fooled. It will revert to letting you sleep, remaining oblivious to your dreams. If you say you want to know your dreams, but you won't write them down, you are not being truthful. This is taken into account by your subconscious and your most dominant picture or desire will manifest. So, give thought to the commitment involved. When you are ready to begin your adventure into dreams, you will have the discipline to wake up and write them down. You can also record dreams by talking into a tape recorder if that is easier or more convenient for you.

Synopsis

- The reason we don't remember dreams is that, in the past, we didn't understand the language of dreams and got bored with them. Through lack of desire and interest, we blocked the memory of our dreams.
- We can reprogram the subconscious mind to present dreams to the conscious mind and awaken us to record them. This is done with consistency and discipline. Reprogramming must be accompanied by an action, such as placing a pen and paper next to the bed. This reinforces the concept of remembering dreams.
- Dream memories are lost quickly upon awakening because dreams are experienced in the subconscious mind. When awake, we experience on a different level of mind: the conscious mind. We can catch dreams if we quickly write them down upon awakening.

Chapter 6

How to Interpret Your Dreams

People communicate ideas using words. However, words are only sounds indicating a specific picture or symbol. The meaning is not in the word alone but in the meaning the individual attaches to it. For instance, it would be hard to identify a *Mugwump* if you had never seen or experienced one. In this case, the word as a symbol is meaningless to you. Another word, such as *peace*, might unfold a series of pictures, meanings, and even feelings because you have placed within your subconscious various ideas relating to that word.

So, words can be seen as seeds of ideas. For example, an acorn is an actual seed that unleashes a mighty oak tree. Within the acorn exists the complete design and potential of a mature oak tree, including every branch, leaf, bark, root, and seed.

A word can represent many concepts, too. A bridge can represent a transition point in life or a crossing from one place to the next. A bridge can indicate moving from the old to a new way, path, belief, behavior, or experience. Death can signify the release of an old way, an aspect of self, a habit, or an idea. It means completed, finished.

When people begin a path of enlightenment, they are often confronted with death dreams. The reason is simple: they are dying to their old selves. Thus, aspects or characteristics of their former selves no longer exist; they have died. It could be that in their old selves, they were judgmental or angry. As they grew, they realized they had no need to be angry or judge anyone and so they stopped.

Dream language is also composed of symbols that translate into ideas. These symbols are often presented as pictures or images, but can also be sensations and thoughts that have meaning to the dreamer. Just as words may have a strict and broad or extended meaning, so do symbols. For example, the word "tornado" refers to a phenomenon of nature, a strong and potentially destructive wind. By extension, tornado as a symbol implies strong, swirling thoughts that are potentially dangerous or destructive.

The subconscious mind presents symbols that are easily understood by the dreamer. It uses images familiar to the dreamer. Once the symbols are translated into words, the interpretation can come relatively easily. This is simply the process of learning a new language. It is the picture language, the language of the subconscious, intuitive mind.

There is a saying that a picture is worth a thousand words. This particularly bears out when working with dreams. As you stand back and look at the canvas of the dream, many things become readily apparent. For instance, is this a scary or humorous scene? Are the individuals portrayed as angry, joyous, friendly, or sad? Are the objects in the dream useful, obsolete, dangerous, efficient, or exaggerated? Much information can be obtained from a quick scan. Then you can move into more in-depth probing.

Symbols also vary in meaning from person to person, depending on one's previous experience with the symbol. (Refer back to the "dog" example given earlier.) For instance, guns are terrifying for many people. The symbol of a gun in a dream might be construed as signaling imminent danger. On the other hand, there are those who love guns and consider them friendly and protective. For these, a dream that includes a gun might indicate either a desire for protection or something else more specific to the dreamer.

Because guns are powerful devices of potential violence or change, they can cause a situation to adjust instantly and radically. Hence, they might be considered a symbol for causing change. I have concluded that the symbol of a gun generally signifies the threat of immediate or even violent change. This may denote the threat of pressure one feels when needing to make a decision that will potentially alter a person's life. This could also be like "being under the gun." With each symbol comes the dreamer's need to evaluate the thoughts and feelings about how the symbol is reflecting that person's world.

Dreams are mirrors of one's waking thoughts, feelings, and actions. Therefore, symbolic meanings are shaded by their context within the dream. For this reason, only the dreamer can completely understand the dreams. Consequently, it is essential that the dreamer unlock the mystery of symbols by asking, "What does this dream mean to me?"

Two Rules About Dreams

There are two rules one must consider when working with dreams. 1) The dream is always about the dreamer, and 2) everyone and everything in the dream represents a part or aspect of the dreamer. By looking at each dream from this perspective, each symbol takes on great significance. That means the tree is an aspect of sturdiness or growth; the water is a quality of fluidity or emotion; the bird is a thought in flight; money represents value; a crabby Aunt Lulu illustrates a crabby self; and an accommodating friend, Hazel, characterizes an accommodating self, etc.

A case in point would be clothing. Clothing signifies the way we present ourselves to the world: our outer presentation. Are the clothes in the dream presented as stylish or out of date? Are you presenting yourself in life in a contemporary, up-to-date manner? Or are you behind the times and out of style? In other words, are you old and foggy in your opinions and notions as you interact with the world?

Furthermore, are the clothes clean and well-kept or frayed, torn, and needing repair? Are you attentive and mannerly in your presentation? Or are you requiring some work and freshening up?

Are the clothes new, worn, shabby, colorful, or drab? For work or dress? Appropriate or inappropriate to the occasion? Every detail is important in the dream, especially the feelings. The feelings illustrated in the dream reveal the dreamer's feelings about the situation.

Here is a sample dream from a female dreamer: *I am at a party and am dressed inappropriately. Other women are attired in formal gowns, and I am nude to the waist and wearing casual clothes. I don't feel embarrassed but I do notice the difference.*

Interpretation: The dreamer is casual in her presentation to the world. Her breasts, being uncovered, indicate she is openly nurturing in her demeanor. Even though she is not embarrassed about her openness, she does feel that it doesn't necessarily fit. Her assumption is that she is expected to be more formal in her life situation. Formality does not feel natural to her. The dreamer commented that she is indeed casual and nurturing in her world, and that there are moments she feels inappropriate because she is unabashedly open.

Since the rule is that everyone in the dream is a reflection of the dreamer, we must examine each person in the dream as representing a specific quality possessed by the dreamer. This includes people in the dream who are not recognizable or are unknown to the dreamer. These people would exemplify parts of self that is not yet known or recognizable.

Also, take note of age, gender, and role within the dream. People of the same gender as the dreamer denote conscious mind aspects. By the same token, the opposite gender signifies aspects of the subconscious mind.

Think of how electricity moves through the wires of a building. There is a push and a pull to the current. The same is true of the mind. Conscious and subconscious minds express in concert, connection, and flow, pushing and pulling energy into expression.

Babies indicate new ideas, ways or attitudes, while young children represent immaturity or qualities that are not fully developed. Children could mean a particular way of thinking or expressing oneself or lack of cultivation. Teenagers suggest more development, yet not fully matured. What does this individual represent? An idea, way of behaving, or quality of self that needs refinement?

Old people indicate wisdom that is accrued through experience and growth. One's parents signify the Superconscious Mind. This is because the parents, whether positive or negative influences in a person's life, illustrate the first and primary authority figures. The Superconscious Mind is the Inner Authority. That being said, a learned person or wise teacher can also represent the Superconscious Mind, the deepest authority. The dreamer always signifies the conscious mind.

Synopsis

- Words indicate specific pictures, symbols and meanings depending on the dreamer's attachment to the word.
- Dreams are presented in picture language, which is the language of the subconscious mind. This mind presents pictures or symbols with which the dreamer is familiar.
- You are actually learning a new language as you decipher dreams. It gets easier as you feel each dream and symbol.
- You can receive an initial impression of a dream by standing back and scanning it like a canvas, taking in the feeling content as well as the general message.
- The meanings of symbols may vary from person to person, depending on the individual's accumulated experiences and understandings and how they interpreted these experiences. Some will see victimhood in an event while someone else will recognize opportunity. Therefore, only the dreamer can completely unlock the mystery of a dream.
- The two rules concerning dreams are: 1) The dream is always about the dreamer. 2) Everyone and everything in the dream represents a part, a quality, or an aspect of the dreamer.
- It is necessary to take note of all factors relating to each symbol since everything adds to the ultimate meaning.

Chapter 7

Symbols Are Quick References

Symbols are a part of our everyday experience. If you were to look out from where you're standing right now, you would see a great number of symbols. For instance, a chair symbolizes a place to sit and rest; a book illustrates knowledge; kitchen, a place to prepare food; food is something ingested and processed, which relates to knowledge that is also taken in and processed. A school indicates a place to learn; a telephone refers to communication; trees relate to growth and stability; a red light means stop, etc. You get the idea.

Think of your dream as a canvas. The subconscious mind is painting a picture on this canvas and each thing in the dream is a symbol denoting something specific to the dreamer. As you become objective (remove emotional meanings), you can step back and observe the dream as a picture and the message can become clear. Ask yourself: *What does this picture say to me? As I gaze at this picture, what feeling does it evoke?* These questions help the dreamer internalize the message of the dream.

Each dream sets the stage for communication between minds by using symbols that are readily understood and familiar to the dreamer. If you are an engineer, your dreams will use terms and examples from your engineering mindset. As a nurse, you will dream symbols that show up in your healing profession, and so on and so forth.

The easiest way to relate to symbols is to use logic. By asking what this symbol means to you, you open your mind to answers. For example, a steamroller is a mighty piece of equipment. Its weight and power can squash everything in its path. If this symbol appears in your dream, you would have to consider the possibility that you might be squashing things or people in your life. Or, you might feel squashed. Another potential is that the steamroller is creating an even-playing field. Take note of the condition of the steamroller. Is it at rest or running? In control or out of control? Are you driving it or is a particular aspect of yourself in charge: conscious or subconscious? Are you happy about the situation or not? Through this type of self-questioning and logic, the answers become clear and the meaning apparent.

Let's consider some symbols that have universal implications.

Universal Symbols

Vehicles

In our world, a car is commonly used as a vehicle to get from one place to another. In a dream, a car could represent some sort of vehicle other than a car that the dreamer is using to get from one place to another. A job is a vehicle to supply income or experience. A class or course of study serves as a vehicle to supply knowledge. A business, hobby, relationship, religious organization, club, civic community, or social group are all different types of vehicles. All serve specific purposes and each assist as you move through life. Even the physical body is a vehicle. It carries you from birth to death.

In your dream, notice the qualities of the car. Is it in good repair or bad? Bright or drab? Efficient, in control? Manageable or not, old or new, etc.? This information sheds light on the nature of the vehicle and whether or not it is serving you well at this time.

Other vehicles experienced in a dream are boats, often seen as emotional vehicles because of their movement on the water; airplanes can be mental vehicles indicating thoughts or ideas; trains or busses can represent organizations or groups of people because they hold many people at the same time; bicycles and motorcycles can signify balance; trucks might represent "work" vehicles.

To extend this idea of vehicles, consider the types of vehicles one would use in other parts of the world. For instance, one might use an elephant, llama, or donkey in an undeveloped part of India, South America, or Africa.

Buildings and Structures

A building represents the mind or a specific state of consciousness. Hospitals would signify healing consciousness. Churches, synagogues, and temples denote spiritual or religious consciousness. Department stores house many diverse items, so they may symbolize Universal Mind, which holds all things. Gas stations would represent recharging or re-energizing yourself with fuel, whether that be inspiration, energy, companionship, or food. The state of learning is illustrated by schools.

A house is also a building and, generally, it has a personal association to you. Your house illustrates your personal state of consciousness. The house you grew up in might be a symbol that would represent the state of consciousness of your family as you developed as a child. For instance, the house I grew up in represents stability to me. From my view, it was a stable, traditional family and I experienced a stable childhood.

Each room suggests different mental activities. The living room indicates the normal daily activities of living; the bathroom is a place of elimination and cleansing; the kitchen, a place to prepare food, which indicates knowledge; the bedroom, a place for sexual activity (unity) or rest. Generally, a bed signifies the subconscious mind as you use it to sleep. Closets suggest ideas or qualities or experiences that are stored or hidden.

The levels of a house refer to various parts or levels of the mind. The first floor or ground level is the conscious or awake mind; the second floor is the subconscious mind; the third floor or attic is the Superconscious or Divine Mind. The basement or cellar represents the hidden mind, the unconscious part of the conscious mind, that part of a person that is repressed or hidden from the dreamer but, nevertheless, affects the physical life behaviors and attitudes.

Other Symbols

Doors, passageways, stairways, hallways and bridges suggest transition. All are objects that allow you to move from one place to the next. The presence or absence of furniture, as well as the condition, symbolizes the quality of thoughts in your mind.

Animals do not possess the ability to reason. They function instinctively and are compulsive in their behaviors. Habits represent the same type of compulsiveness, so animals in dreams denote habits of the dreamer. Note the nature, quality and condition of the animal. To illustrate, a rabbit might represent procreation or creativity; insects can be insidious, pesky habits; dogs indicate friendship or viciousness, depending on the dreamer's perspective; cats might reflect secrecy or independence; bears could represent possessiveness, mothering, or smothering. Age-old universal animal symbols include a horse, which represents will (used for work); a snake might indicate wisdom; fish could represent spirituality.

In a dream, sexual intercourse represents a union between two parts of the mind. Typically, male and female unions symbolize the connectedness and harmony of conscious and subconscious minds. If sex is conducted between two people of the same gender, it denotes union of either two conscious aspects or two subconscious aspects. Marriage signifies a state of harmony, oneness, and working together of the conscious and subconscious minds.

Water is another common symbol. It relates to life in the physical world. So, if it is raining, the illustration is being made that, in your conscious experience, you are feeling that life is coming down on you. If you are drowning in a dream, your life experience is overwhelming you.

Why are dreams presented in symbols as opposed to words? Because our experiences are conducted primarily in the physical world, and we usually identify with it. Often, we define ourselves based on where we live, our friends, type of career, house, and the car we own. We rate ourselves on performance, rate of pay, status, and physical image, like beauty. Because of this close association with the physical world and the limitation it imposes, the most efficient way for the subconscious mind to communicate with the conscious mind is by use of physical pictures or symbols familiar to the conscious mind.

The way we relate to the material world directly matches the manner in which the subconscious relays information in the dream state. Again, a picture is worth a thousand words. One single picture recalled from the dream state is easier to decipher than 1,000 words. Pictures are truly a universal language and override language barriers. Of equal importance is the fact that the conscious mind is more likely to accept emotionally loaded messages in symbol form than if presented literally.

When you are deciphering the meanings of symbols in your dreams, ask yourself questions. If a *place* is predominant in the dream, ask, "Why do I go there?

What is the purpose for me? What feeling do I get from it?" If the dream presents a person, ask, "What do they represent in my life?" People in dreams always represent aspects of the dreamer. This refers to qualities, ways of thinking, behavior, etc. Describe their qualities. This will help you know how the place or person relates to *you*.

Always reason with the symbols to allow their meanings unlock for you.

Dream Symbols and Their Meanings

Accident: Something unexpected or being out of control

Afternoon: Middle of a cycle

Air: Thoughts

Animals: Habits or compulsive behaviors; look at the type of animal and temperament.

- Cat: Independence, possibly secrecy
- Bear: Hibernation, reclusiveness, power, possessiveness, mothering
- Beaver: Time for action; to build something
- Buffalo: Abundance (American Indian lore)
- Butterfly: Transformation
- Deer: Gentleness (American Indian Lore)
- Dog: Pals, friendship, loyalty; or vicious, rabid, a pack animal
- Elk: Strength, nobility, longevity
- Fish: Spirituality or spiritual knowledge
- Fox: Crafty
- Horse: Will power, work (as a plow horse), power
- Insect: Pesky insidious habit; an ant might mean industriousness
- Mouse: Focus and attention to details (American Indian lore)
- Mule: Stubbornness
- Rabbit: Procreation, creativity, or timidity
- Raccoon: A need to cloister, become reclusive; stay back and observe
- Snake: Wisdom, creative energy, kundalini, healing energy (caduceus)
- Wolf: Teacher (American Indian lore)

Armed Services: Regimentation, disciplined action

Birds: Thoughts (fly in the air) Notes: American Indians saw birds as God's messengers

- Dove: Peaceful thoughts
- Eagle: Strength or vision
- Hawk: Visionary
- Cardinal: Creativity

  Vulture: Scavenger-type thoughts

  Chicken or Turkey: Limited thinking (can't fly)

Birth: Beginning of a cycle; a new beginning; initiation

Blood: Life Force; element of joy

Body parts: Vehicle through life. Note what each part represents

  Breasts: Nurturing quality

  Ears: Hearing, receptivity

  Eyes: Sight, perception, vision

  Feet: Spiritual foundation or foundational values

  Face: Identity

  Hair: Conscious thoughts: groomed, tangled, dirty

  Hands Activity and purpose in life

  Heart: Center of self, love, knowing (*I know it in my heart.*)

  Joints: Flexibility

  Legs: Movement forward

  Mouth: Expression

  Nose: Identity

  Penis: Creativity

  Shoulders: Carrying burdens

Books: Knowledge

Bridge: Transition in life, moving to a new way, belief, or experience

Buildings: States of consciousness

  Church, Synagogue, Temple: Spiritual consciousness, spirituality

  Department Store: Universal mind (can find anything there)

  Garage: Storage for vehicle

  Gas Station: Recharging, reenergizing

  Hospital: Healing

  House: The mind/personal state of consciousness (see House)

  School: Learning

Chair: Place to rest, be stationary

Choking: Trying to take in too much or choking on an idea or expression

Circus, Carnival: Way of life; fun, games; chaos; a lot happening at once

Clock: Time

Clothing: Outer presentation, way you present yourself to the world
Clouds: Thought forms
Colors: Each color has a vibratory frequency or quality of energy
- Black: Quietness, death, lack of stimulation, the unknown
- Blue: Peace
- Brown: Earth, nature, grounded
- Green: Healing, growth
- Gold, Silver: Something valuable
- Grey: Illness, neutrality, something wrong, possible negativity
- Orange: Energy, excitement
- Pink: Love
- Purple: Royalty, Highest Energy, intuition
- Red: Intense emotion (anger, enthusiasm)
- White: Purity, completeness
- Yellow: Happy, mental acuity, intellect

Computer: Brain
Costume: Pretending to be something
Dam: Holding back, being blocked
Dancing: Harmony
Dark: Unknown, without understanding, possible dread
Death: Transition, change, release of old aspects, completion of old ways
Direction: Where you are going
- Left: The past, receptivity, feminine energy
- Right: The future, masculine energy
- Up: Higher consciousness, reaching for more, moving higher
- Down: Lower or deeper vibration

Door: Transition; portal of change or transition
Driving: You are in control
Drowning: Feeling overwhelmed
Fighting: Conflict; fighting life
Fire: Purification
Food: Knowledge (note the type: junk food, nutritious food)
Furniture: The way you furnish your mind, thoughts, beliefs, attitudes and style

Garage: Storage for vehicle (body?), place to store junk
Green Light: Go
Gun: Quick change, pressure to make decision
Hair: Thoughts
Hallways: Transition from one thing to another
House: The mind, dreamer's personal state of consciousness

    Basement, Cellar: Unconscious mind, hidden or stored issues: fear, guilt, prejudices, misunderstandings; buried hopes, dreams, and aspirations

    First floor: Conscious mind, awake mind

    Second floor: Subconscious mind

    Third Floor: Superconscious Mind, Higher Self, Divine Mind

    Attic: Higher Consciousness, Superconscious Mind

    Roof: Higher Self, Superconscious Mind

    Room: A specific mental activity (see Rooms)

Hurricane: Uncontrolled, destructive thoughts
Ice: Frozen, static, stagnant life experience
Intersection/Fork in Road: Decision time
Jewelry: Value, adornment
Knife: Cutting thoughts, cutting through or away
Lake: Contained life experience, potentially emotional
Left: Past, receptivity, feminine energy
Light: Awareness, enlightenment
Mail: Communication
Makeup (as in cosmetics): Covering up, beautifying
Mask: Disguising self, hiding
Marriage: Union, harmony, commitment,
Mirror: Looking at self
Money: Value, personal value
Morning: Beginning of cycle
Mountain High place, a goal, or an obstacle
Movies: Imagination, visualization
Mud: Change manifesting in life
Music: Harmony, unless it is disharmonious

Newspaper:	The news, what's going on
Night:	End of a cycle, darkness, unaware or unknown
Nudity:	Open, honest, vulnerable, nothing to hide
Numbers:	Each number is a symbol and has a value
1:	Beginning, initiating force
2:	Duality, decisions, opposites
3:	Expression
4:	Stability
5:	Change; reasoning capacity
6:	Service, nurturing
7:	Quietness, introspection; meditation
8:	Power, energy, money or value
9:	Completion of a cycle, spirituality
10:	Initiation, beginnings that have power (0 adds power to any number)
11:	Mastery
22:	Mastery
33:	Mastery
Ocean:	Universal Mind
Outside:	The outer world
Paint:	Covering up, up-dating, improving
Parent:	Authority, Superconscious Mind, High Self
Party:	Happy, party atmosphere, social activities
Path:	Path in life
People:	Aspects of the dreamer. Describe the person as a quality or energy. People of the same gender as the dreamer represent the conscious mind; the opposite gender represents the subconscious mind.
Actor:	Pretending
Babies:	New ideas, new ways or attitudes
Children:	Immaturity, qualities not fully developed
Clergy:	Also, priest, minister, rabbi, monk: spiritual teacher, leader
Doctor, Nurse:	Healing aspect
Dreamer (You):	The conscious mind
Elderly Person:	Wisdom

Parents: Highest authority, High Self, Divine Mind.
    Mother: Receptive aspect
    Father: Aggressive aspect
Police: Discipline and/or regimentation
President: Highest authority
Teacher: An authority figure
Teenager: Somewhat developed but not fully matured
Unknown Person: Unfamiliar or unknown aspect of self

Pool: Contained body of water, would relate to a specific life experience
Purse: Personal identity and value
Radio: Communication, possibly news, depends on how you use it
Rain: Life flowing, life coming at you
Right: Future, masculine energy or action
Ring: Commitment
River: Natural flow of life
Road: Pathway in life
Rooms: Mental activities
    Bathroom: Purification and cleaning, release
        Toilet: Release
    Bedroom: Mind at rest, subconscious mind
        Bed: Subconscious mind
    Closet: Hidden or stored ideas, qualities, or experiences
    Dining Room: Place to take in or assimilate knowledge, social gatherings
    Kitchen: Place to prepare, serve knowledge (food)
    Living Room: Where and how you consciously live, normal daily activities
Sex: Union of conscious and subconscious minds, harmony
Singing: Harmony
Sky: Mind
Snow: Frozen or static situation, paralyzed
Socks: Protection for spiritual foundation (feet)
Stairway: Changing levels of consciousness; transcending; transition
Stop sign: STOP
Storm: Conflict, inundated with life experiences

Street: Path in life

Telegraph: Communication

Telephone: Communication

Television: Imagination, visualization

Tornado: Energy out of control, destructive thoughts

Trees, Plants: Growth

Vehicles: Specific vehicle being used: an attitude, organization, job, career, organization, or physical body.

    Airplane: Thoughts, ideals, philosophies

    Bicycle: Balance

    Boat: Emotional vehicle

    Body: Your container

    Bulldozer: Pushing things around; destroying or preparing for new construction; reshaping the terrain

    Bus: Organization or group

    Car: Your personal vehicle, possibly your physical body

    Motorcycle: Balance

    Steamroller: Squashing things or people, being squashed, creating an even-playing field

    Train: Organization or group vehicle

    Truck: Work

Wallet: Value, identity

Water: Life experience, possibly an emotional element

Wedding: Union, harmony

Wind: Movement of thoughts

Windows: Perception, clarity, "seeing," becoming aware

List Your Personal Symbols Here

More Personal Symbols

Archetypal Patterns Are Also Symbols

Another type of symbolism is archetypes. Archetypes are energy guides that show up in your life as ingrained, innate tendencies. They are energy patterns that reveal the role(s) you are to play. One of the ways you will discover them is as symbols in your dreams.

Each person came into this lifetime with a team of archetypal guides: the roles one is to play and the lessons one is to learn. These are natural behavioral traits that emerge in the personality, like default systems. When you understand your own archetypal tendencies, you will notice them regularly showing up in various situations. You will begin to recognize other people's patterns as well.

For many years, I have had dreams of hanging out with the president of the United States, whichever one was currently serving. Does that mean that I am to be the president? No! It means I have an archetypal pattern of expressing my highest authority (symbolized by the president of the United States, the highest authority in the land). As I reflect on the day prior to having this dream, I notice that I have been in situations where I have been speaking from my highest authority as a teacher, speaker, or in some other manner of communication. My dream reflects that situation.

Let's look at some common archetypes.

An individual may play the *hero* or the *victim*. One person may demonstrate *hero* behavior to the thundering applause of others. Applause and spotlights may be required, or just show up naturally. Another person may be a *hero* by going quietly about his business and helping people in difficult circumstances. This individual's sense of fulfillment and personal gratification from providing service to fellow humans is reward enough. This is not to disclaim enjoying applause or recognition.

The implication is that each person will play his role according to his own personal evolution. Perhaps the highest form of *hero* is to be of great service. This could be through inspiring entertainment or quiet action behind the scenes. These patterns are an individual concern. One must ask in earnest, "Can I use this pattern in a positive way?"

The goal, once we understand our archetypal guides, is to rise to the highest energy expression of that pattern. In my case, it would be to serve students and clients by speaking truth with highest authority. In all cases, the point is to bring to awareness the fact that these energy patterns are symbolic. They recur in our lives to help us identify what we are to express, how we are to grow, and why certain situations tend to repeat.

If you have a *teacher* or *child* image appearing in your dreams, it will prompt you to see a pattern you came in to fulfill. Recognizing these archetypes helps you to know why you respond to situations as you do and why certain behaviors are natural to you. Soon, you will recognize how you are to grow.

Some people are natural *leaders, teachers,* or *coaches* and others are *caregivers, scientists, creatives, magicians,* or *warriors*. Still others are *business aficionados, musicians, tech wizards*, or *sports stars* from the word go. These patterns are divinely placed to guide each person to live his purpose. Even in malevolent patterns, there are seeds of greatness.

The task is to acknowledge the pattern, overcome whatever weakness is indicated, and work to bring its divine potential to light. For instance, if one has a *victim* archetype, the energy pattern can be explored. It might indicate that the individual can evolve from feeling sorry for self to becoming compassionate toward other's plights. In so doing, this person can cultivate this pattern into its highest energy form.

A *queen* or *king* archetype can demonstrate a benevolent leader, ruler, or boss, present to help his constituents or underlings. Or one of these archetypes can exhibit an angry, impatient, off-with-your-head mentality.

The same is true of all archetypal or symbolic patterns: one either expresses divine potential or weakness. It is a choice that reflects personal development. When you use these energies to their highest capacity, you are living your purpose.

Therefore, don't be shocked if a *rock star* persona shows up in your dreams and you find you are often center-stage in a *rock star* position. If that happens, use your *rock star* status well.

Don't be surprised if a person with an *engineer* archetypal pattern regularly finds himself in situations that require his unique problem-solving abilities or engineer's viewpoint. This can be said of the person with a *mother* archetype who continually finds herself nurturing, nursing, or caregiving. There is the *trickster* who tricks and manipulates others or himself, for good or evil.

The *actor* might find himself in situations where he is playing a role with costume and script in hand. This could play out as one acting in a production, acting in a role as a salesperson or politician, or simply pretending to be something one is not. This is not to indicate that all salespeople or politicians are acting, but as leaders, they all have moments of taking the stage. These roles come forward consciously or unconsciously. There is an advantage to recognizing what comes naturally and to shape it into something that serves benevolently.

There is a theory that everyone has a *bully* archetype. We often notice this in the way people bully themselves and create self-esteem issues. If one can spot this *bully* energy, one can transform it into *collaborator, teacher, leader,* or even *visionary.*

Another example is the *warrior* archetype, which can be seen in a *soldier, reformer,* or a *transformer.* As a *reformer,* one can fight an unfair system or sponsor changes that benefit everyone. Or the *warrior* can spend his life fighting everyone and everything. It is all in how this energy is directed.

Some of my personal archetypes are *teacher, healer,* and *psychic.* These are the dominant patterns presenting in just about everything I have done in life. My work and yours is to develop these patterns into their highest expression.

It won't be hard to recognize these energy patterns because they present themselves often. In a particular situation, you may find yourself stepping up to take charge as a *leader,* or shrinking back to be invisible like the *wallflower* or the *victim.* They will show themselves in dreams. If you find you are always teaching in your dreams, you are a *teacher.*

Here are a few more archetypes you may recognize: *child, orphan, white knight, beggar, addict,* and *servant.* A *prostitute* means giving away your values and morals for an easier way. The *saboteur* indicates destroying the old for the new. What symbols are presenting in your life?

Again, the Universe guides us with its symbolic language. It is a gift to understand its messages as we are continually shown the way. Many people search for purpose: *Why am I here? What am I supposed to do?* By looking with symbolic eyes, answers are provided. That is the gift of archetypes, symbolism, and dreams. The Hindu holy book, The Bhagavad Gita, suggests we live our purpose (dharma) to the best of our abilities. By examining the symbols that show up in our lives, we bring light to the big picture, the wholeness of who we are, and we discover the direction that is always before us.

The purpose of offering this information on archetypes in this book is to bring to light the symbolic nature of your internal behavior patterns. It is true that everything in material life is a symbol, and all symbols point the way to our highest use of energy and potential.

Synopsis

- Everything in life is a symbol that can be understood. The object or event's symbolic value relates to its function and purpose.
- To interpret a symbol, ask questions: What does this object/picture speak to me? What is its purpose? What feeling does it evoke? What quality or qualities does that person represent? Use logic to decipher the meanings.
- As one looks at the dream picture being painted on the canvas of the mind, one can develop objectivity. By standing back impartially, the meaning becomes apparent.
- Everything about the symbol has significance: color, number, condition, type of vehicle, level of the building, type of animal, gender and temperament.
- There are Universal symbols: cars as vehicles through life; houses as the individual's personal state of consciousness; buildings as mind; animals as habits; water as conscious life experience, etc.
- The subconscious mind uses symbols familiar to the dreamer. Pictures are succinct and override language barriers.

Chapter 8

Four-Step Formula for Easy Interpretation

Now we are ready to move on to the dream interpretation formula. There are four steps to understanding dreams.

Step One: Feeling

State the predominant feeling of the dream. If there is more than one feeling, indicate the feelings in chronological order. (Tip: keep this simple.)

Step Two: Theme

Note where the dream takes place. How is the stage set? Where the dream takes place tells you what part of the dreamer's life is being commented on.

- Outside, at a party, carnival: a comment *on* your view of your conscious experience of you in the world
- In your house: your state of consciousness
- In a building: note the particular purpose or use of the building
- At work: relates to your state of mind at your job or career
- A road: concerns your path in life
- In a hospital: about healing
- Church, synagogue, temple: concerns your spirituality or growth
- School: relates to what you are currently learning
- Funerals and death: changes occurring in your life and what you are releasing
- Weddings: unions or commitments with the self

- Births: new ideas or ways you are developing to live life

Step Three: Symbols

Go over the symbols given in the dream and interpret each one. List these in chronological order.

Step Four: Conclusion

To arrive at a conclusion, you must put Steps One, Two, and Three together in sentence- or paragraph form. The conclusion is about *you*. Start it with, "I am ___(feeling)___ about ____(theme)____." Follow this with the symbols. Place the symbols and their interpretations in chronological order and in sentence-form.

This conclusion simply restates the dream message in words. So, in fact, you are interpreting picture language into English language. The dream makes a statement. The dreamer interprets the statement and determines how it fits the dreamer's life. It is important to relate the dream statement back to the experience of the day previous to the dream to find connections.

Interpretation in Action—Making It Work

Using the above method to interpret actual dreams, here are some examples from real people. We will walk through the interpretation process and check with the dreamer to see how the dreamer correlates the dream to the life experience.

Dream A (Female)

I am in a large school and I'm lost. I've lost my class schedule and don't know where I'm supposed to be, but I know that I'm late to class. I feel panicky and confused.

Step One: Feeling - panicky and confused

Step Two: Theme - school/learning situation

Step Three: Symbols

school = a learning situation

student = dreamer

class schedule = timetable of lessons

Step Four: Conclusion - *I feel panicky and confused about my lessons in life. I don't know where I'm supposed to be or what lessons I'm supposed to be learning. I feel pressured and feel that I am behind time or late.*

Relevance: In this dream, the dreamer confirmed that she was feeling confused and unclear about what she was to be learning from her experience. She felt she was missing the point. This dream offered an opportunity to see clearly what was happening so the dreamer could make some decisions about moving forward.

By the way, this dream is common to many people. I've heard it in many formats. The dreamer shows up for football practice all suited-up and he doesn't have the play list for the game. The dreamer shows up for class and the professor calls on him for a report and he has no clue what he is supposed to report on. Same theme, different dreamer. All reflect a sense of being unprepared and confused about where they are in life and what to do next.

Dream B (Female; I am following up with the same type of dream.)

I am lost in a school and end up in the video room. In the room, I see a girl and two boys. The girl jumps out the window of the room and is hurt but survives just fine. The boys remain in the room. Then it starts raining.

Step One: Feelings - lost

Step Two: Theme - school/video room (imagination, use of the mind)

Step Three: Symbols

    school = learning situation

    video room = imagination

    window = perception

    girl = conscious self

    boys = subconscious self

    two = decision

    window = perception

    rain = life experience

Step Four: Conclusion - *I feel lost as I deal with my imagination. I am crashing through to a new perception. I am injured, but just fine.*

In this dream, the dreamer is learning (school) about her imagination (the way she is using her imagination and perceiving life). She is consciously (girl) crashing through an old perception and, even though she is hurt, she is just fine. Subconsciously, she is dealing with a decision (two). Then it rains meaning that she is in her life experience.

Relevance: The dreamer had just found out she was unexpectantly pregnant. She had basically crashed through old perceptions of family and come out a bit hurt, but fine. She adjusted her view about having a child (crashing through the window) and she was dealing with a new subconscious decision (two) that she had held subconsciously (boys). It is all about her life experience (rain).

Dream C (Male)

I am in school and intent on taking a written exam. I cover my paper with writing and feel pretty good. The instructor (former female teacher) informed me that the answers were incorrect but she liked the way I filled the paper.

Step One: Feelings - feeling pretty good

Step Two: Theme - school/learning

Step Three: Symbols

> self = the dreamer
>
> female instructor = subconscious authority
>
> exam = a test determining his understanding about life
>
> answers = incorrect; understanding is not complete or correct
>
> liked the way paper was written = inner authority was pleased with efforts in physical life
>
> filling the page = lots of activity

Step Four: Conclusion - *I feel focused and good about my learning situation. My inner subconscious authority is letting me know that my conclusions are not correct but my effort is good.*

Relevance: The dreamer compared this information to what he was doing the day of the dream and determined that he was attempting to learn about life and his conclusions might have been lacking.

Dream D (Female)

I am walking alone on a train track and hear the train approaching. I feel fear and start to run along the track. The train is bearing down on me. It appears it will run me down. Then I decide to turn and face the train fearlessly to stop the train with my arm outstretched. I do this and the train stops. I feel proud of myself.

Step One: Feelings - fear and intimidation, which changes to courage and pride

Step Two: Theme - the path of life (train tracks) which seem predetermined

Step Three: Symbols

    train track = pathway of life already set up

    train = large vehicle, possibly organization or family

    outstretched arm = purposeful confrontation

    facing the train = standing up to the organization

Step Four: Conclusion - *I am alone on my path in life. The path seems predetermined or laid out for me. An organizational vehicle is bearing down on me and appears it will destroy me. So, I decide to confront it and it stops. I am proud of myself for my courage.*

The dreamer confirmed that she was involved in a large organization that demanded more and more of her. She finally bravely confronted the person in charge and the pressure was relieved.

Dream E (Female)

I am squeezing white heads on my face. As they break, a stream of white material shoots out. It looks like a white noodle. There is a plate full of these noodle-like things. I am intent on doing this.

Step One: Feelings - intent and focused

Step Two: Theme - dealing with identity (face)

Step Three: Symbols

    face = identity

    white heads = blemishes on identity

    white material = impurities being expelled

    plate full of white material = many impurities

Step Four: Conclusion - *I am intently working on my identity by pressing out or releasing my impurities. There are a many blemishes and impurities that are being released.*

This person is in counseling and focused on changing her attitude about the way she deals with situations. She is intent to "clean up her act." She felt the dream illustrated her determination to change for the better.

Dream F (Female)

I am in a movie theatre with two friends, Doreen and Darlene (made up names). We all go to the bathroom. It takes me a long time to release. We are in different stalls laughing throughout this time. By the time I finish, Doreen and Darlene are outside waiting. They left their purses inside the bathroom.

Step One: Feelings - fun, laughter

Step Two: Theme - this is about the use of imagination or visualization (movie) and cleansing and release (bathroom)

Step Three: Symbols

movie theatre = the way imagination is used

Doreen = conscious aspect representing security (per dreamer)

Darlene = conscious aspect representing strength

bathroom = place to release impurities

purse = identity and value

Step Four: Conclusion - *I am having fun using my imagination. I am releasing old ideas with the assistance of my sense of security and strength. My identity and value are lodged in this release (bathroom).*

Again, this individual is going through counseling to let go of old ideas and attitudes. She is aware of her personal strength and security. She is enjoying the process and building value. Her personal identity and value (purse) are connected with this release.

Dream G (Female)

Michael and I have a cute, fat, happy baby girl. I am trying to find socks for her and clothes for both of us so we can get dressed and go. Someone said to the baby's dad, "I owe you a lot of money."

Step One: Feeling - searching

Step Two: Theme - new idea or new way in life

Step Three: Symbols

Michael = subconscious quality representing love and helpfulness dreamer = conscious self

baby = a new beginning or new way in life

socks = protection for spiritual foundation (feet)

clothes = how self and new way is presented in the world

Michael (dad) = subconscious self

money = value is coming with this new way

Step Four: Conclusion - *I am searching for protection for my new spiritual way or my new spiritual idea. The subconscious quality of love and helpfulness and conscious self are working together to present this beautiful, happy, conscious new way to the world. My subconscious is informing me that much value is attributed to this new beginning.*

This individual is learning to meditate and tune in to the subconscious mind. She is calmer and feels more connected spiritually because of her efforts. She is in process of learning how to present this new side of herself to others, but feels she has been guided by her subconscious to meditation. It has added great value to her.

Dream H (Male)

It is morning. I'm in a large city that I am familiar with but I am nevertheless confused because the street signs are missing. I know I'm headed for the train station. I am riding in a red car that is self-propelled. I meet a former female teacher and she asks what I'm doing. I reply that I'm learning Latin. Then I find the car has stopped and I am pushing it from behind.

Step One: Feeling - confused

Step Two: Theme - traveling the road of life to get to a group/organization

Step Three: Symbols

morning = beginning of cycle

large city = large state of consciousness, busy

missing street signs = lack of direction

train station = meeting place for large group/organization

red car = emotional vehicle, anger, enthusiasm?

Latin = ancient language (dreamer's definition)

female teacher = subconscious authority, wisdom

Step Four: Conclusion - *I am confused. I am traveling my path and familiar* *with where I am, which is vast and busy, but don't know how to reach my designated destination, which is a group or organization. I am beginning a new cycle (morning). I feel emotional and self-propelled. I meet a subconscious, authoritative, wise aspect that questions what I am doing. I respond that I am learning an ancient language. When I realize this, my vehicle is no longer self-propelled and I must now push it.*

The dreamer is a student who is beginning to learn something he was originally excited about and then found to be of no relevance (ancient). His inner authority is questioning this and he is having to push himself to continue studying. His object is to get to school (train) but he feels directionless at the time.

Dream I (Male)

I'm driving my car down a mountain road. The road is curvy and the descent is faster and faster. I am frightened and losing control.

Step One: Feeling - frightened, losing control

Step Two: Theme - traveling on a high path in life

Step Three: Symbols

    car = vehicle through life

    mountain = high place or large obstacle

    mountain road = high path

Step Four: Conclusion - *I am frightened and feel out of control as I come down from a high place. I do not feel in control as I move along the twists and turns of my life path. It seems dangerous. I seem to be coming down (descending) too fast.*

The dreamer is a recovering alcoholic and reports having this dream during the time he was an alcoholic and feeling out-of-control when he was coming down from an alcoholic high.

Dream J (Male)

I am in the basement going through a maze of hallways and doors trying to get upstairs. It seems to take a long time to get through and find the way upstairs.

Step One: Feeling - confused, lost, determined

Step Two: Theme - lost in a maze in the unconscious

Step Three: Symbols

> basement = unconscious part of mind
>
> hallways, doors = transitions
>
> upstairs (from basement) = conscious mind

Step Four: Conclusion - *I am confused and seem to be wandering through a maze of unconscious issues: fear and guilt issues. I keep making transitions and finally move to a conscious state.*

Here, the dreamer is trying to sort out lots of past issues and is making changes as he goes. He wants to make his growth conscious and practical.

Dream K (Male)

A foreign army is chasing me. The soldiers are shooting at me and trying to kill him. I am running and terrified.

Step One: Feeling - terrified

Step Two: Theme - trying to escape conflict

Step Three: Symbols

> foreign army = many unknown aspects at war with self
>
> soldiers = conscious aspect, combative
>
> dreamer = conscious self
>
> shooting guns = attempt to change violently

Step Four: Conclusion - *I am terrified and in conflict, which seems large and foreign to me. I feel threatened and I am trying to run for it while being fired upon. (This could also mean being yelled at, criticized, or attacked.)*

The dreamer reports that he is working with the police to bring down a drug ring. He is aware of the danger he is in and wants to run.

Dream M

I am in a car with my father. I approach a bridge. I am afraid and don't want to cross the bridge. My father drives the car across the bridge.

Step One: Feeling - fear, hesitancy

Step Two: Theme - the road/path of life, transition

Step Three: Symbols

> father = high self, divine mind

bridge = transition

self = conscious self

Step Four: Conclusion - *I am afraid as I travel the road of life and reach a transition point. My Higher Mind is with me along the way and takes control of my vehicle and gets me through the transition.*

The dreamer started a new job with much apprehension. She prayed and was able to make the adjustment.

Dream N (Male)

I am at a costume party. Everyone is wearing a costume and a mask except me. I wander around, observing. It doesn't bother me that I am different from them.

Step One: Feelings - curiosity, observing, enjoyment

Step Two: Theme - costume party, how dreamer sees life

Step Three: Symbols

costume party = presenting self in a made-up way

party = fun energy

costume and mask = disguising self

Step Four: Conclusion - *I am in life observing, feeling curious, and enjoying things. Aspects of myself are masked and hidden, presented as something different from what they are. I feel fully present and aware of myself. My ability to be in observation mode makes me different. I don't mind that at all.*

This person feels that to play the game of life you have to present yourself in different ways and play various roles. He feels fine about this.

Dream O (Female)

We are in a small town. Jack is the minister. I am waiting for him calmly. He arrives and I am asked to walk across the room doing "dance forward step" I am wearing a strapless dress that is very loose. I am uncomfortable. I walk across the room and sit down.

Step One: Feelings - uncomfortable and waiting

Step Two: Theme - small part of self

Step Three: Symbols

small town = small consciousness

Jack = subconscious aspect representing insecurity

minister = spiritual teacher

strapless dress = uncomfortable in outer presentation

"dance forward step" = maneuvering as if dancing forward

Step Four: Conclusion - *I am in a small state of consciousness, waiting and feeling uncomfortable. A subconscious insecure aspect (dreamer's interpretation) presents himself as a spiritual teacher to me. He directs me to perform and present myself as moving forward. I do this, but do not feel secure or comfortable in my presentation. I complete my duty and retire.*

The individual states that she is feeling uncomfortable about what she has been presented as spiritual teachings. It doesn't fit well for her. She has been waiting for something better to show itself. But presently, she feels she is simply performing according to direction and is uncomfortable and insecure about it.

Dream P (Female: This was a nightmare.)

I was visiting cousins in a large, institutional house. They had two tigers and two black pumas wandering around the house leisurely. I was a little frightened of them, but figured that if I moved slowly and quietly, they wouldn't harm me. However, one of the tigers was closely following around my youngest brother (a child in my dream) and growling at him. I was frightened for him, so I would shove him into a bathroom or other room and shut the doors so the tiger couldn't get to him. But it seemed like the doors were always opening. The tiger was persistent. I finally carried my brother down a long hall to an auditorium and shut the glass doors to keep out the tiger.

Step One: Feelings - frightened and protective

Step Two: Theme - large institutional house

Step Three: Symbols

large institutional house = a large dogmatic mindset

two = decision to be made

tigers and pumas = danger, ominous

youngest brother = subconscious developing aspect, vulnerability

doors = transition points

hallway = transition

Step Four: Conclusion - *I am feeling frightened in a large, dogmatic, institutional type of mindset. There was danger threatening. I tried to assume a low profile to deal with the danger. Then the danger sought out a subconscious, developing part of myself. I kept trying to protect this, but no matter, it was always visible and vulnerable. Finally, I transitioned and closed off this vulnerable part of myself. I shut down.*

The dreamer had left a large dogmatic religion (institution) and felt vulnerable as though she could be attacked at any time. She was trying to keep a low profile and hiding the fact that she was developing in a new way. She thought that being reserved and hiding made her less vulnerable. The whole idea of leaving a religious path that had been drilled into her mindset for her whole life was frightening, but the dream showed her determination to let new ideas develop and to protect her new way in life.

Dream Q (Female: This is a similar dream as remembered from childhood. It shows that big cats—pumas, lions, and tigers—can represent fear, which seems big and life-threatening.)

I was sitting on a chair in the house where I grew up My mother was combing my hair. There was a big hole in the wall. I could see a big lion sitting across the street, waiting for me to leave for school so that it could eat me. I was terrified.

Step One: Feelings - terrified

Step Two: Theme - state of consciousness of family (childhood house)

Step Three: Symbols

> mother = high self (saw her mother as indoctrinated by rules and not living her life as a free being; that is how she saw God: dictatorial and dangerous)
>
> childhood house = state of consciousness in her family of regimentation and following outside authority's rules
>
> hair = thoughts
>
> combing air = grooming thoughts
>
> hole in wall = space with a wall/obstruction that allowed her to see
>
> lion = danger

Step Four: Conclusion - *My higher mind is grooming my thoughts. There is danger outside a wall I have maintained. The wall is not that protective* *because there is an opening (hole) in it, which means I am open to see beyond the wall that was being erected. There is a dangerous behavior or habit (lion) that is waiting to eat me.*

This lady was indoctrinated and groomed with religious dogma. But there was an opening in her thinking. She felt that this openness made her vulnerable to being attacked. The person who regularly attacked her was herself. She wasn't buying into all the beliefs of others, and that made her feel vulnerable and open to attack, mostly from herself. She was only six years old at the time.

Dream, R (Female)

I am with my daughter and her baby. My daughter is frustrated, impatient, and pushy. I am feeding her baby large pieces of noodles. I keep trying to stuff more noodles into the baby and the baby is choking because she can't take in anymore.

Step One: Feeling - frustrated, pushing

Step Two: Theme - new idea being overfed

Step Three: Symbols

    oldest daughter = demanding, pushy, and impatient

    baby = new way in life

    large pieces of noodles = food/knowledge

    choking = trying to take in too much

Step Four: Conclusion - *My impatient, demanding self has a new way in life, and I am trying to feed this new way with too much knowledge and overwhelming it.*

Relevance in her words: "I am trying to learn too fast and am overwhelming myself. I need to slow down and calm down and let the new information sink in." Great interpretation.

Dream S (Male)

I am driving down a road that has been washed away and is full of debris, but I make it. There is a jackknifed 16-wheeler laying on the side of the road. The truck driver is okay. A vicious dog is going after two cats in my car, but I get there first and shut the door, keeping the dog out.

Step One: Feeling - danger, threatened

Step Two: Theme - road in life

Step Three: Symbols

    road = pathway in life, how things are unfolding presently

    road washed out and full of debris = path seems unclear and obstructed

        jackknifed truck = work vehicle that is derailed

        truck driver = conscious part of self; he is okay

        vicious dog = dangerous habit

        two = decision

        cats = independence

Step Four: Conclusion - *I feel threatened on my life path. It is obscured and obstructed. Overall, I am okay but feeling in jeopardy, in danger of being attacked. I am able to keep the viciousness at bay and able to protect my independence.*

This man is having trouble with his purpose at work. He states that his path in life seems obscured and he is under attack at work.

Dream T (Male: This dream is yet another version of being lost in life.)

I was going to the golf club to play golf and I couldn't find my tee time. There were golf clubs all over the tee, and it was a mess.

Step One: Feeling - out of control, a mess

Step Two: Theme - golf, the game of life

Step Three: Symbols

    golf club = place where you play the game of life

    tee time = a designated time to join the game of life

    golf clubs = instruments to play the game of life

Step Four: Conclusion - *I want to play the game of life, but I don't know when to do it. I feel overwhelmed and out of control with all the instruments of the game in disarray and all over the place.*

The dreamer is conscious about wanting to play the game of life, but he doesn't know when he is to do it. He says this conclusion of things being in disarray and overwhelming pretty much describes his life.

Dream U (Female)

I am in the mall and there is a man calmly chasing me and telling me that he is going to marry me. I don't know him, and I keep saying, "You're crazy. I am not going to marry you." The people at the mall say, "He is trying to connect with you." He gives me a ring, then we sit on a bed. He is sitting behind me with his arms wrapped around me. I can feel the love coming through me and it feels so good. He says, "This is what it's supposed to be like." The man is Jesus. I feel loved and relieved.

Step One: Feeling - confused and resistant; then loved and relieved

Step Two: Theme: - mall, being chased by man.

Step Three: Symbols

    mall = universal mind (malls have everything in them)

    people = aspects of dreamer

    Jesus = love

    marriage = connection/unity

    ring = commitment

    bed = subconscious mind

Step Four: Conclusion - *I am universal mind (mall). There is a subconscious aspect declaring that we will be connected and unified. In my conscious self, I am confused and resisting. He gives me a ring which represents commitment. Then we sit together on a bed (subconscious level) and connect. He sits behind me with his arms wrapped around my shoulders and tells me that this is what it is supposed be like (to be loved). The man is Jesus (love) and I feel loved and relieved.*

Relevance: The dreamer had been in an abusive marriage for many years. She was trying to understand love and connection. Her conflict came from the belief that men just want sex. This dream helped her to see that more is possible, and that she is loved.

Dream V (Female)

I am pushing food back into the refrigerator. Trying to shove it in as it is overflowing, and I am trying to get the door closed. There is too much food to get into the refrigerator.

Step One: Feeling - struggling, pushing, trying hard to push all the food in

Step Two: Theme - trying to keep all the food preserved and stored

Step Three: Symbols

>house = conscious self
>
>food = knowledge
>
>refrigerator = a place for storage and preservation

Step Four: Conclusion - *I am struggling to fit all of my knowledge into preservation and storage. There is too much knowledge to keep locked away.*

Relevance from the dreamer: "I have been studying spirituality and metaphysics for a long time with a goal of doing tarot card readings. This dream is telling me that I need to start expressing my knowledge instead of trying to keep it shoved inside of me in storage. My knowledge and understanding of spiritual principles are overflowing. My teacher has told me that I am ready to do readings and I need to trust myself. This dream is helping me to do that."

Dream W (Female)

I am on a boat in the ocean with a family: father, mother, and nine-year-old daughter. The young girl is thrown from the boat and is attacked by a huge shark and torn to pieces. I am observing the scene without emotion.

Step One: Feeling - objectively watching

Step Two: Theme - in a vehicle in the vastness of universal mind

Step Three: Symbols

>boat = vehicle
>
>family (mom, dad, daughter) = dreamer sees these people as intellectuals
>
>9-year-old girl = a developing intellectual aspect
>
>shark = a large fish, spirituality

Step Four: Conclusion: *I am in the vastness of universal mind with two mature intellectual aspects and a developing intellectual aspect. I observe as the developing aspect is thrown from my vehicle and destroyed (torn apart) by my large spiritual understanding. I feel no loss in this.*

Relevance: The dreamer has been studying spiritual principles for a long time and actively developing her intuitive faculty. She realizes that the destruction of the young intellectual aspect by a huge body of spiritual knowledge indicates she has made a choice to operate more from intuition that intellect.

Synopsis

- There are four simple steps to interpreting a dream.
- Step One: Denote the *primary feeling quality* of the dream.
- Step Two: Determine the theme. Where does the dream take place? The place relates to the theme of the dream or what part of the dreamer's life is being referred to or commented on.
- Step Three: List and interpret symbols.
- Step Four: Draw a conclusion by writing out the first three steps in sentence form. This indicates the message of the dream.
- After completing Step Four, compare the message of the dream to what was being experienced the day before the dream. This will help to recognize what the dream refers to and the event or circumstance may have a deeper significance.

Chapter 9

Putting It All Together

Sleep comes in stages and cycles. While asleep, a dreamer passes through various levels of sleep. Scientists have determined that dream cycles occur in increments of ninety minutes. When one goes to sleep, he slips gradually into a deep state of slumber for approximately an hour. He gradually lifts himself to shallower sleep for about fifteen minutes. The person then repeats the cycle: deep sleep followed by shallow. The cycle is like a loop. As the dreamer makes this passage, the body becomes still, as if tuned to an inner frequency awaiting a message. It is during this stillness that dreaming occurs.

As the sleeping period wears on, a change is noted: the periods of shallow sleep lengthen and deep sleep shorten. Dreams from deep sleep are hard to recall because, by the time you reach a shallow part, you wake up and have lost their memory. Whereas, shallow sleep dreams are more easily recalled and often appear vivid.

Remember, dreaming is a process by which the subconscious mind communicates with the conscious mind. Dreams offer an objective picture of the day's activities, along with emotional imprints. They are objective, non-judgmental assessments and overviews of the conscious mind's activities and responses during waking hours when the dreamer is operating in the material world.

Often, people are not aware of their attitudes and behaviors, or what they feel as they move through experiences. Therefore, by paying attention to the subjective subconscious assessments in dreams, you can spot areas of challenge, resistance, and opportunity. This feedback provides invaluable information that supports spiritual development.

People may find themselves in situations in their waking life that reflect principles that are difficult to cope with or understand. Dreams provide a fascinating perspective for personal assessment, growth, and enlightenment. They help clarify, simplify, and illuminate.

As we experience in the physical world, our opportunities to learn and grow expand. As we listen to the unconditional insight of the subconscious mind received through dreams, growth becomes easier.

It is said that we attract to us people and situations that have the potential to *teach* us. Often, we find ourselves in encounters and relationships similar to previous ones, apparently repeating patterns. Perhaps we have not learned everything we needed to learn from the past and must once more repeat the experience in order to educate ourselves. Once we have learned the relevant lessons, we do move on to new expanded prospects. Learning in the material world then, becomes our chance to progress and move forward to live fully.

By working with our dreams, we synchronize our conscious and subconscious minds to work together, thereby achieving a state of harmony and strengthened intuition. Instead of fighting life, we greet it with arms wide open. As this interaction becomes more frequent, easier to interpret, less restricted and more fluid, we sustain a greater degree of health and wholeness. The goal is to achieve an awareness of the conscious, subconscious, and Superconscious elements functioning in harmony as one: perfect synchronicity and harmony. Life is good!

Synopsis

- Sleep occurs in stages and cycles: periods of deep sleep followed by shallow sleep. Shallow sleep dreams are the easiest to recall.
- Dreams are commentaries from the subconscious mind to the conscious mind about the previous day's experiences. Therefore, dreams offer a fascinating resource for enlightenment and growth.
- Paying attention to the people-qualities presented in a dream helps one develop and understand oneself.
- Dreams provide a way to check one's progress in life and clarify the lessons one is learning.
- Working with life and learning consciously and voluntarily produces harmony, health, and wholeness. Fighting life results in chaos. The goal is complete alignment of conscious, subconscious, and Superconscious minds.

Chapter 10

Your Life as a Dream—Tools and Exercises

When I work with a client, one of the first things I say is, "Growth is like peeling an onion—one layer at a time. The outer layer is thicker and harder than the inner layers of the onion, so that when each layer is removed, it reveals many interior layers that are soft and juicy."

The point is, growth is a layer by layer proposition. Releasing our outer judgments and beliefs makes inner exploration possible. We have each constructed our own layers (experiences, adventures, reactions, emotions, and beliefs), and it is up to us to peel them away to discover the truth of our being.

The onion analogy is perfect to help understand the complexity of the individual self. Many people spend their entire lives focused on the external world, the hard part of the onion, and never question, Why? *Why am I here? What is this about? What is the purpose of this experience or relationship? Why have I failed? Have I failed?* Regrettably, the rest of the onion, the inner self that offers greater meaning, goes unnoticed.

In that regard, your dreams are invaluable. They give you a chance to become acquainted with your inner essence (intelligence/consciousness) and become "the wise observer."

The observer is that inner essence that travels with you wherever you go, even from lifetime to lifetime. It is truly your authentic self. You might call it the soul. The observer (watcher) is of a higher vibratory quality than the conscious mind, personality, or ego. You could say it has a front-row box seat at the game called your life. You have access to its unerring perceptions.

With any experience, you have the option to become fully engaged (hooked) or stand back and watch. At any time, you can practice being in *observer-mode* when in the company of friends, family, or at work. Just sit back, mentally and emotionally, and notice what's going on. Observe the energy in the room and the interplay of people. Observe your own reactions and judgments. Become familiar with the part of you that has no need to hook into the event or to judge, but simply observes. When you do this, you will have discovered a crucial truth: *What happens to you is not as important as what you do with what happens to you.* To say it another way, the event is not as relevant as how you process it and use the information.

Working with your dreams provides a perfect opportunity to practice observing because dreams show up from an observer's viewpoint. Simply put, your dreams are an objective and subjective record of your life and how you are living it. They are presented in the form of a cinematic story. So, each night, you get to be entertained, or horrified, or informed as you view your dreams.

If you turn off your inner judge, you can observe dreams from a purely detached perspective in the same way you watch a movie. Here is your life in technicolor and dialogue. This is how you really feel about it. This is way better than having twenty witnesses offer their unsolicited opinions, feedback, and advice. The information in your dreams are coming directly from *you*. It is the real thing!

Consider another advantage in developing the ability to understand symbolic-picture-dream language. You can take this premise of symbolic interpretation into your daily awake life.

The four-step interpretation formula is adaptable to your personal experiences on a daily basis. In fact, by applying symbolic interpretation to your awake adventures, you will discover an amazing reflection of where you are caught, where you are stuck, or where you are progressing in your growth and evolution. It is a beautiful, unerring way to receive cheap therapy because dreams never lie. They never paint over something relevant. Dreams, asleep or awake, clarify lessons learned and unlearned. Stepping back and viewing your life in this detached frame, will help you see it all the more clearly.

When you ask yourself why people have different experiences, you will find the answer in their experiences, which are direct reflections of where they are in their growth. Viewing life as a series of symbols that reveal your state of consciousness, is an accurate and effective tool to understand yourself. In fact, it may ultimately be the most important benefit to developing the skill of dream interpretation.

Closed Eye Experiment

It was stated earlier that the subconscious mind communicates through pictures and feelings. There are images and emotions imbedded in every experience and every part of your life. So once again, it is necessary to pay attention and capture all aspects of your waking dream called life.

Let us try a closed-eye experiment to help you try out this new concept. Close your eyes and begin to observe your breathing. Take a few deep inhalations and exhalations. As you do this, pretend you are standing behind your body and observing your lungs and chest expand and deflate.

As you breathe in, imagine you are *drawing in energy*. As you exhale, imagine *tension flowing out from the body*. After several deep breaths, let your breathing return to its normal rhythm, but continue to watch. Notice the rhythm.

The more you can objectively observe your breathing, the easier it will be to detach from your physical body and your day-to-day experiences. You will begin to perceive your life without judgment and become the observer. In time and with practice, you will begin to identify with that silent, knowing part of you that just watches non-judgmentally.

Now, in your mind's eye (imagination), see the muscles of your body becoming very relaxed and placid. Continue this relaxed breathing until you feel comfortable, calm, and peaceful.

Let your mind drift back to a recent experience of the past year; one that was significant to you. This can be either joyful and exciting or unpleasant and painful, or anything in-between. As you view the experience, relive it in its entirety in your imagination, noting the people, circumstances, and emotions, particularly your own. Flow through the event chronologically, observing how you dealt with it and the outcome. While still relaxed and calm, note your impressions of the people, the nature of the experience, and your feelings concerning the way you handled it. Record these impressions in your mind.

Now, begin bringing your attention back to your physical body and the present moment. Do this by feeling your feet grounded to the floor and your body grounded to the chair in which you are sitting. Take in a deep breath and open your eyes. (It may be helpful to record this excursion on an audible recording device so that you can follow along in a relaxed state with your eyes closed.)

Quickly describe the experience on paper. Do this as though you are recording a dream. Include and list in your recollection the people involved in the incident and your impression of them. Each person represents an aspect of yourself. List the other symbols and their meanings. When you have completed these preliminaries, use the four-step interpretation formula.

Here are some examples:

Experience A (Recorded by a young male; names are made up.)

A good friend of mine, Tim, committed suicide by shooting himself with a gun. At the time, he lived with his dad. His mother was deceased. He was very close to his mother and missed her. This was one of the reasons he killed himself: he missed his mother. In a note, he left his coin collection (his only valuable) to his best friend, Joe, who I didn't know. I was shocked at how quickly life can end. This was the first of three violent deaths in my immediate neighborhood. I also felt very disturbed that Tim couldn't work out his sadness.

Step One: Feelings - sorrow, shock, disturbed

Step Two: Theme - death/transition/change

Step Three: Symbols

> Tim = friend, kind, caring, conscious aspect
>
> Tim's dad = good, kind, mature, conscious aspect
>
> Joe = decent, good friend
>
> gun = tool for violent change, decision to move on
>
> coin collection = value

Step Four: Conclusion - *I feel shock, sorrow, and disturbed by a quick, violent change occurring within a kind, caring part of my conscious self. A decision was made and the transition was accomplished violently. As a result, there was value left behind that was transferred to another decent part of self. The value* *that was passed on is an appreciation for life and its fragility. The underlying factor leading to change is a desire for closeness with the nurturing quality of the Superconscious Mind (mother).*

The individual who recalled this experience admitted not liking or wanting change and fearing mortality. Therefore, a violent transition of the type described made a deep impression on him. The value that was passed from Tim to Joe was, for symbolic purposes, transferred from one conscious aspect to another. The value (appreciation for life) is now a part of the conscious mind, whereas before the experience, appreciation may not have existed. The person recalling these events notes that this incident occurred during a time of family problems and the threat of moving was looming. So, this individual was going through fear and perhaps depression on some level. The situation involving his friend made a strong point to him that was needed at that time: the value of life. That is why this particular memory came to him during this exercise.

Experience B: (Recorded by a female)

I was in a hurry to get home after shopping. I was driving my car as I left the shopping center. I was behind another car and looking to the left (as I was going to turn right) waiting for an opening to pull out onto the road. There was a gap in traffic (to me it seemed like a long gap). I assumed the car in front of me pulled out. (I did not look to confirm this). I saw another lull in traffic and put my foot on the gas to pull out and hit the car in front of me that had not moved nor taken advantage of either gap in traffic to pull out to the road. The other driver, a female, and I pulled over and exchanged numbers. It did not appear to me at that time that either vehicle was damaged, but I found out later that both vehicles were damaged slightly.

Step One: Feelings - anxious and impatient to get on the road of life, and to get home (spiritual center)

Step Two: Theme - the road of life (the dreamer's path)

Step Three: Symbols

driving = in control

road = path of life

car = vehicle through life

break in traffic = opportunity to move out

> damage to vehicles = path endangered
>
> shopping center = Universal Mind
>
> the other vehicle = obstacle; possibly another person
>
> other driver = unknown conscious aspect not grasping opportunities to move ahead

Step Four: Conclusion - *I am anxious and impatient. I want to get on the road of life (my path) and return home to my spiritual center after experiencing Universal Mind – vastness of life. I am impatiently attempting to move on my path, but I'm obstructed by another vehicle (person?). An unknown conscious aspect that does not appear to be interested in opportunities for movement, obstructs my path. I smash into the obstacle. It appears that there is no damage to either one of us, yet there actually is damage to both. (Impatience can lead to emotional/mental/physical damage.)*

The individual who reports this accident perceives her lessons to concern patience and trust. She has a strong desire to progress on her path in life and often feels obstructed. Sometimes, the obstruction feels like another person. She does get caught in the past (left) and looking to the future (right) and forgets to be in the moment (seeing directly ahead). She wants to progress faster. Her impatience sometimes keeps her from seeing the full picture of what is going on around her. This event indicates that the obstacle is an unknown conscious part of herself. (Impatience? Looking at the past and the future?) She rushes into situations without having the full view of what she is getting into. This impulsiveness creates problems for her. She admits to having, at times, aggressively pushed things out of her way, rather than dealing with them more personally. She acknowledges that there must be a conscious part of herself that wants to go slow but finds it annoying.

Experience C (Recorded by a female)

I was walking my friend's dog and stopped at my daughter's house. As I entered the house, I called out to my daughter, "Hello." I had just stepped in the door when she yelled, "No, no." With that, a large dog she had been taking care of came charging to the door and attacked my little dog. My daughter was screaming as I tried to open the big dog's jaws and pull him off my little dog. As we got the small dog out of the death grip of the large dog, I escaped my daughter's house. We were all traumatized (me, my daughter, and my little dog). I called my male friend for help but he refused to come and help with the wounded dog, even though the dog belonged to him.

Step One: Feeling - open and friendly, then fearful, traumatized, and shocked

Step Two: Theme - innocently walking my path in life with my habitual pattern of friendliness and sweetness

Step Three: Symbols

    small dog = habit of sweetness, innocence, friendliness

    large dog = (represents owner) habit of being stuck in his ways, holding on with determination

    daughter = open, efficient, kind, helpful, love

    friend = stubborn, self-absorbed, stuck in his ways, holding on

Step Four: Conclusion - *I am feeling friendly as I walk my path in life with my habitual behavior of being open and innocent. My pattern of being sweet, open, and innocent (small dog) is attacked by another behavioral habit (big dog) that represents being stuck in my ways and holding viciously onto the old. My innocence could have been destroyed had it not been for the part of me that is efficient, loving, and interceding (daughter). I was traumatized by what seemed like a shocking situation. I am waking up to the danger and viciousness of my old ways of being stuck and holding on to things past their time of usefulness.*

Relevance: The person who experienced this event realized that she had a habit of innocently staying in a relationship with a person who was not showing up for her. This person was self-absorbed and stubbornly stuck in his ways, and she had regularly made excuses for him.

The universe showed her, through the trauma and drama of this life event, that her boyfriend (whom she had telephoned for assistance) would not offer support or help with the small, injured dog (that actually belonged to him). He was stuck in his selfishness and she knew it was time to end the relationship. She acquiesced to the notion that things had to be dramatic and obvious before she would have made that decision.

Experience D (Recorded by a female: Here, the student used the formula to

understand her habitual feelings of uneasiness and edginess that she should be doing something she was not doing at the moment. She flashed back to an experience from the past that seemed relevant.)

I am a child, standing in line in an all-girl's convent boarding school. I turn to the child behind me and I say something. We laugh. A nun comes up behind me and slaps me hard across the face. I feel shocked, confused, and humiliated in front of the other girls. I feel guilty that I did not obey the rules (that I did not intentionally break) and displeased the nun. I now stand in line with straight posture and stoically look straight ahead.

Step One: Feeling - shock, humiliation, guilt

Step Two: Theme - convent boarding school, lessons about spiritual self

Step Three: Symbols

    boarding school = learning encompasses lessons (school) that deal with life experiences (room and board) of a religious nature (convent)

    nun = conscious self; dogmatic, religious aspects; religious teacher

    female children = conscious aspects being developed, not yet mature

    lined up = rules, restraints, expectations, "toe the line" (dreamer's interpretation)

    speak out = expressing self

    laughter = expressing fun part of self

    attacked from behind = unconscious, hidden thoughts make themselves known

    slap across face = identity violently attacked

    stand in line, facing ahead = keeping the rules, identity focused forward

    stoic = turn off emotions, hide behind emotions

Step Four: Conclusion - *I feel shocked and confused about the life lessons that are upon me. The conscious aspects of me (girls) are in the process of developing (children) in regard to religious elements (convent school) that deal with rules and restraints (standing in line). My natural expression of self (speaking, laughing) is attacked and dominated by unconscious thoughts (hidden behind me) of religious, dogmatic authority (nun). When I express myself and have fun, I violently attack my own identity with confusion and guilt, creating second-thoughts about my actions, like I should have known to* *do something else. I see my own spiritual authority as being overruled by punishment and the demands of authority figures. I turn off my emotions (stoically) and create a new identity (facing forward) that plays into the expectations and demands of others for fear of being humiliated and attacked again.*

Student's evaluation: "Seeing the words *identity violently attacked* made a big impact on me. It struck me that I gave up my spiritual authority by identifying with dogma and religious concepts that centered around a mean authoritarian god with lots of rules that weren't clear and didn't even make sense. A god that would trick me and come up behind me with terrifying surprises that made me *on edge all the time*. No matter what I did, it *could* be wrong. No matter what I said, it *could* be wrong. No matter how I acted, it *could* be foolish and unacceptable. I could be punished at any moment. On top of that, *they* said god is love. So here is this loving god that had hell waiting for me in the corner. I could get thrown into hell for doing something I didn't even know was wrong.

"Wow, these thoughts directly relate to my *feeling on-edge for no reason at all*. Over the years, I have worked through many dogmatic issues, many misconceptions of god, many methods to identify my own authority, etc. I find peace in this understanding. If in the future, I am aware that I am feeling edgy about something unknown I'm supposed to be doing, I can refocus myself to my true freedom. I am my own authority. The only power *behind me* is my own true Self."

Making It Real—More Tools and Exercises

There are other ways to use dream symbology as a practical tool for gaining insight into yourself and your evolution in life. Here are several exercises to aid you in self-assessment.

Exercise I: Family Constellation

Make a list of family members and other important people in your life (employer, employees, friends, neighbors, clients, teachers, etc.). Beside each name, list the main quality represented by the person. List the first thing that comes to you. Don't think too much about it.

For instance, if the attitude or behavior that resonates the loudest about the individual is generosity, use that as the descriptive quality portrayed by that person as a symbol to you. If you have difficulty determining the primary characteristic of a person, describe that person as you would if you were speaking to another individual. To illustrate, you might say Charlie seems "happy, humorous, and good natured." These descriptive words form the meaning Charlie represents for you and translate into a symbol in your life.

There is a saying that you see in others what you yourself possess. The concept of dream interpretation is based on this truth.

Fill out the chart on the next page with people you know. Identify the name of the person and relationship to you. List the qualities of that person. Note if the person is a conscious or subconscious aspect. For males, other males represent a conscious aspect and females represent a subconscious aspect; vice versa for females. Maturity Level: adult is a mature aspect; adolescent is a developing aspect; baby is a new aspect or new idea. I've included an example in the chart.

Name of Person	Qualities of Person	Conscious or Subconscious Aspect	Maturity Level
Example: Anna, sister	good natured, happy, humorous	conscious aspect (from a female)	mature aspect (Anna is an adult)

To process this list, note if there are similar qualities listed. You might have indicated a number of honest (or possibly dishonest) people in your life. This would mean that you are learning about honesty and perhaps expressing yourself honestly (or dishonestly). The attributes you listed about these relevant individuals relate directly back to you. Understand, however, that you may not be expressing the quality in the same manner as the people noted. For instance, you may be honest to others but extremely self-deceptive.

Observe and register the qualities that stand out in the people you relate to most. Keep this sheet for use as a dream interpretation tool. More than likely, these individuals may appear regularly in your dreams.

To learn more from this exercise, on the next page list people who were prominent in your life ten years ago, then twenty years ago. Recognize the movement of your life. Are your lessons different now than they were ten or twenty years ago? Are you concentrating on the same issues or different ones? Do you have a clear perception of the qualities of the people in your life? Are you even aware of the type of people you are dealing with? If not, why not? You can gain much personal insight from processing this exercise.

(Note: A person's qualities may change over time. People do change and your perception of them also deepens and develops over time.)

Name of Person	Qualities of Person	Conscious or Subconscious Aspect	Maturity Level

Exercise 11 Becoming Objective

Look back to the time when you were approximately seven years of age. Describe your family as you perceived each individual. List one to four qualities that best describe their attitudes, beliefs, and behavior (according to your perception). Include stepparents as well.

Step One: Make a list of the members of your family of origin.

Family Members	Most Dominant (Obvious) Qualities
Example: Mother	Fearful or nurturing or martyr or critical or resourceful, helpful or creative, etc.

Step Two: The circle on the next page represents your family. You will be placing, inside or outside the circle, X's to represent the various members of your family of origin: mother, father, sisters, brothers, and others who may have lived with you or been very instrumental in your childhood.

Note that in the center of the circle, there is an X. Next to the X, begin by writing the name of the person who seemed (from your perception) to be the most dominant person in your family of origin. The one who seemed to rule. If your mother was the dominant personality in your household, put her name and qualities by the X in the center of the circle. If the family revolved more around your dad's influence, then his name goes in the center.

Step Three: Next, place an X with a name and quality inside or outside the circle to represent each member of the family listed above. Place these X's close to or far away from the original X (the most dominant person) in relationship to how close each person seems in your perception to be connected to that dominant member.

Example: If your mother was the most dominant person in your family, the center X will represent her energy. If your sister was very close to your mother, place her X near the center X, which represents your mother. Continue to place the X's around the circle in relationship to each person's position with the dominant family member.

When you finish placing your various family members in and around the circle, draw an X for yourself to represent your relative position in the family.

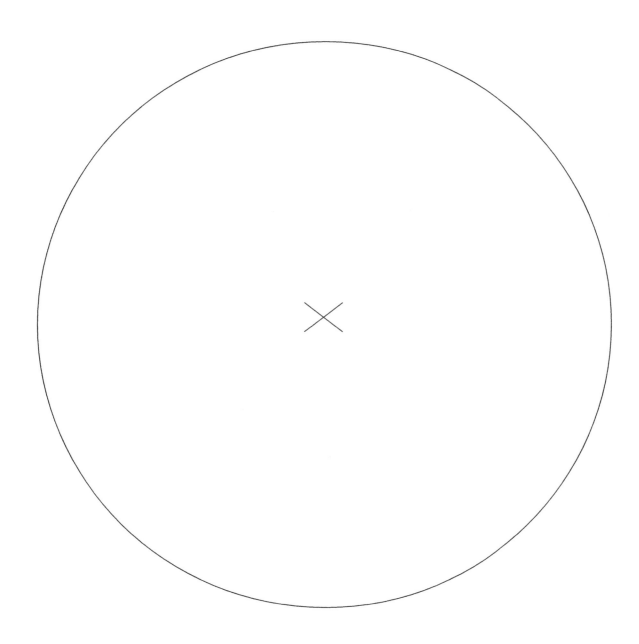

Most dominant person in my family of origin: _____

His/her quality/qualities: _____

Step Four: Answer the following questions:

What are your observations about your family?

What are the most dominant or repeated qualities?

What is the main theme (dynamic) in your family?

What type of power dynamic existed in your family of origin?

What were the "family secrets"? What things were known within the family but never talked about? Example: No one talked about emotions. The fact that grandmother helped out financially was not discussed. An illegitimate child or abortion in the family was "off-base" for discussion.

Conclusions:

Exercise III: Family as Reflection

Now, look at the diagram in a different way. If you remove the names of the people from this drawing, the Family Constellation illustrates many qualities. Some of the qualities are very dominant and others are not so dominant (those removed from the center of the circle), but they are present and important. This entire circle, with all of the qualities noted within it, represents *You*. These qualities suggest the lessons that you came into this life to learn and develop in a positive way. The dominant quality symbolizes a most important and valuable lesson. The other qualities refer to parts of you that are less dominant, yet still important.

You function as each of these people at various times. More than likely, you express their particular qualities in a way that is different from how they expressed it. For example, rigidity can be viewed as closed-mindedness, fear, an attempt to control, or potential determination, etc. You possess all of these qualities in some form or capacity. It is your assignment to learn to express them well and as constructively as possible. As you progress, you express these qualities in more productive ways. It is called growth.

If there is a negative quality listed, understand that your challenge will be to turn it into something positive. Each characteristic has a positive and a negative side to it. Stubbornness can be converted to perseverance; over-sensitivity can become empathy and compassion; passivity can be transmuted into taking time for self-reflection; criticalness can be transformed into discernment; and over-responsibility for others can be turned into responsibility for Self.

What are your observations about how the qualities of your family of origin play out in your life?

Exercise IV: Present Day Life

Using the same format as the "Family Constellation," construct another Family Constellation using the people that are currently in your life. These are the folks you presently associate with. They can be neighbors, business associates, children, friends, etc.

Extended Family Members	Most Dominant (Obvious) Qualities

Now, starting with the person most dominant in your life in this group, place X's for these people around the circle. Include the names and qualities next to each X.

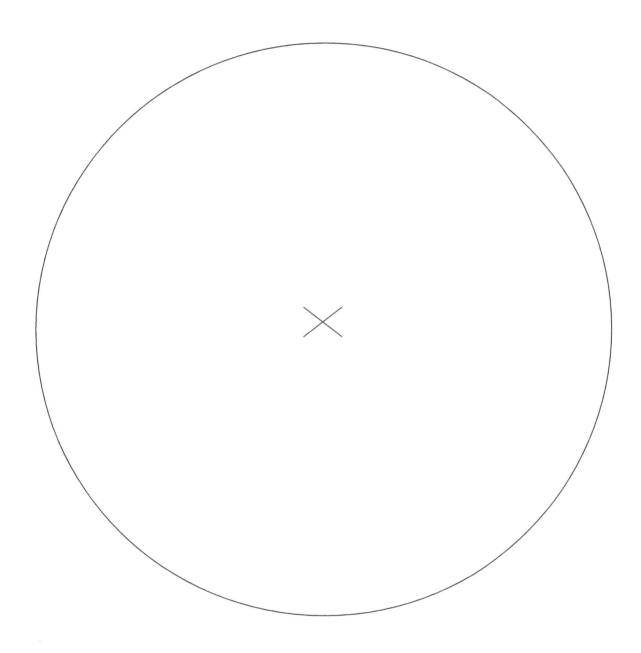

Most dominant person in my current <u>extended</u> family: _____

Qualities of this person: _____

Now remove the names but keep the qualities in the circle. Compare this diagram with the previous one.

Are there repeated qualities? What are they?

Are you focusing on different lessons or the same ones?

Have you renamed the original qualities? Are they more positive, negative, or about the same as before?

Do you denote movement or evolution in your life journey or not?

You can chart your progress by using these exercises. The important point to remember is that everyone in your life represents something within yourself: a quality, characteristic, desire, etc. We know this to be true because, if we were to name a famous person, such as Mohandas Gandhi, Oprah Winfrey, or Stalin, we can find descriptions to identify their personalities or what they represent to us. For example, Oprah Winfrey might be identified as rich, expressive, caring, incest-survivor, one who found her own way in life. Each descriptive word may reflect a different meaning for the observer. In turn, the observer uses that individual and representative quality as an internal symbol relevant to the self.

Often, you have the same lessons appearing again and again in life. This is considered the cycle of life. You are ever learning about life and refining yourself through the experience. When you find that you are experiencing the same situation or lesson, or going through the same experience again, understand that it is a refinement of yet another level of the original lesson. Repetition does not necessarily mean that you have not progressed. There is much depth of understanding to be achieved in the repetition, just as there are many levels to any particular lesson. Much can be accomplished by concentrating on one area of improvement. Remember, all lessons and experiences are important and necessary to self-development.

If you follow these guidelines, you will soon be able to objectively recognize a pattern in your life. By monitoring the intuitive energy of dreams, you will learn to identify more quickly the pattern you are dealing with and opportunities for growth. Understanding dreams will deepen your intuition. You will know instinctively what a situation offers and how you can grow within it.

There are truly no negatives in life. Every situation is neutral. It is what you do with your experiences and how you react to them that counts. Reactions say more about you than they do about the circumstances. By observing situations, you learn more about yourself and those around you. Self-control develops naturally.

Synopsis

- Personal and spiritual growth can be compared to peeling an onion; it is a layer-by-layer proposition.
- We have constructed our own layers (experiences, adventures, reactions, emotions, and beliefs) based on our conclusions about any situation. It is up to us to discover what these layers are and make adjustments as needed.
- Dreams reveal a glimpse of our authentic self because they occur when there are no pretenses: at night when the day is done and our conscious minds are at rest.
- At any time, we can step back and view an experience from our feeling-sensing mind. We can understand more conclusively its relevance by using the Four-Step Formula.
- This process is adaptable to everyday situations. It can be used to decipher our lives in greater detail and depth to discover the lessons and opportunities at hand.
- There are various ways to use dream symbolism as a practical tool for gaining insight into ourselves and our paths of evolution in life. The Family Constellation is a tool to use to map our soul progression.
- It is helpful to look symbolically at the people in our lives: family, friends, business associates. This practice aids us by helping us perceive our primary lessons and the qualities we are developing at any given point.
- From time to time, we can use the Family Constellation exercise to check our progress, note changes in our developing awareness, and see the patterns we are attracting.

Chapter 11

Holy Books Written in Symbolic Language

The Bible

All these lessons Jesus taught the crowds in the form of parables. He spoke to them in parables only to fulfill what had been said through the prophet: "I will open my mouth in parables, I will announce what has lain hidden since the creation of the world." Matthew 13:34-35

What we utter is God's wisdom, a mysterious, a hidden wisdom. God planned it before all ages for our glory. None of the rulers of this age knew the mystery; if they had known it, they would never have crucified the Lord of glory. Of this wisdom it is written: "Eye has not seen, ear has not heard, nor has it so much as dawned on man what God has prepared for those who love him." I Corinthians 2:7-8.

These are but a couple of references in the Bible about hidden wisdom. As we deal with biblical allegory, we are instructed to look beyond literal translations of the words to discover a deeper meaning or reality. There is indeed hidden wisdom in each passage and story, and it is available to us as we look with different eyes and listen with receptive ears.

The Bible, the Bhagavad Gita, and other "holy" books speak in allegory and parable for those who are ready to receive their wisdom. As we apply symbolic language to these works, we draw forth significance applicable to current life experiences.

Following are some clues on how to accomplish this.

1. Look at biblical events as not only historical in nature, but also as experiences within you as an individual. Ask yourself, "How does this story describe what occurs within me as I grow spiritually." By looking with curiosity and openness, you will discover that many of the stories illustrate stages in your personal evolution.

In the story of the crucifixion, Judas betrayed Jesus for a few pieces of gold. Jesus symbolizes mastery, higher consciousness, the Christ energy. In the story, it appeared that Judas (ego or materiality) sold out Jesus (Christ energy) for a few pieces of gold (small value) as he presented the Christ to the Roman soldiers (regimentation according to the old law).

The theme of this story represents the struggle between the materialistic ego and the higher mind of love. Jesus always lived from a higher perspective. He symbolizes higher consciousness (the goal). In the encounter in Gethsemane, when Jesus surrendered to the soldiers, his actions illustrated that you don't fight materiality; you move beyond it. He taught us how to live in love. (*Forgive them for they know not what they do.*) This experience alludes to letting go of struggle and ideas of limitation in order to move to a higher dimension of spiritual love.

It appeared that the Christ was destroyed, but not really, as Jesus returned from the dead (as the Christ always will) to continue teaching those who were willing to hear and see with new faculties. The crucifixion of Jesus might indicate the giving up or surrender of personal ego and limiting ideas that keep us stuck. We can claim our own sonship to the divine by letting go of base energy to rise up to our higher power.

Jesus (mastership, love, Christ Self) showed us how we are to take up our cross (learn the temporal lessons of ego) and transcend the material world (limitation, chaos, and conflict). The bigger lesson is about love.

As a result of these events, Judas committed suicide (ego relinquishing its hold). The individual moves out of an egocentric state of consciousness into a higher awareness of sonship. He does this by recognizing the folly of buying into the false belief of money having more value than love, or, placing a material focus above the finer essence of Christhood. He essentially supplanted earthly focus with a higher realization of spiritual life.

Does this sound like you?

2. View the names of people in the Bible as giving clues for what each represents as far as aspects, qualities, or characteristics of self. By knowing something

of the character's expression, you can delineate the quality it refers to. The Hebrew or Arabic meaning of the name will also supply insight. An example would be the name *Jesus*.

In Hebrew, Jesus means *whose help Jehovah (God) is deliverance, safety, salvation, savior, helper, prosperer, deliverance through Jehovah.* Matthew 1:23 states, *The Virgin shall be with child and give birth to a son, and they shall call him "Emmanuel," a name which means "God is with us."* So, to arrive at the quality represented by Jesus, we would combine these ideas and state simply that Jesus signifies God within who delivers and saves us from the limitations of our own thoughts.

3. Names of places are also symbolic and indicate locations in the mind as well as states of consciousness. In that regard, consider Jerusalem, a Hebrew word for *habitation of peace, dwelling place of peace, possession of peace.* The consciousness of Jerusalem would be a state of peace.

4. Numbers play a significant role in interpretation throughout the Bible. Refer to the symbolism of numbers in the chapter on dream symbology.

5. While studying the Bible in its symbolic form, look for key words as symbols. Be careful not to get so caught up in each detail that you miss the forest for the tree and forego the deeper meaning. Look at the stories as pictures to be interpreted as a dream. It is helpful to summarize each paragraph, story, or chapter to arrive at the larger picture.

6. Have fun with the process. There is great joy in realizing the messages that provide a new narrative and a higher message. Learning in this way can be freeing and joyful!

Reading the Symbols—The Birth of Jesus

To commit the information on symbolism to practical application, let's consider a story recorded in the Bible about the birth of Jesus. As you read this biblical description, imagine you are listening to a dream. By the way, the Arabic, Greek, and Hebrew interpretations of specific names in this section are taken from the *Metaphysical Bible Dictionary* published by Unity School of Christianity, Unity

Village, Missouri.

Now this is how the birth of Jesus Christ came about. When his mother, Mary was engaged to Joseph, but before they lived together, she was found with child through the power of the Holy Spirit. Joseph her husband, an upright man unwilling to expose her to the law, decided to divorce her quietly. Such was his intention when suddenly the angel of the Lord appeared in a dream and said to him: "Joseph, son of David, have no fear about taking Mary as your wife. It is by the Holy Spirit that she has conceived this child. She is to have a son and you are to name him Jesus because he will save his people from their sins." All this happened to fulfill what the Lord had said through the prophet: "The virgin shall be with child and give birth to a son, and they shall call him Emmanuel," a name which means 'God is with us.'" When Joseph awoke, he did as the angel of the Lord had directed him and received her into his home as his wife. He had no relations with her at any time before she bore a son, whom he named Jesus. Matthew 1:18-23.

Now, let's use the Four-Step Formula to interpret the symbols in the text.

Step One: Feelings - first shame and denial, then acceptance

Step Two: Theme - a birth, new beginning accompanied by guidance and direction from an angel

Step Three: Symbols

    birth = starting something new, a beginning

    baby = a new part of self, a new beginning (see *baby* below)

    Mary = love and intuition (see *Mary* below)

    Joseph = increase and imagination (see *Joseph* below)

    angel = messenger from God (see *angel* below)

Before moving to Step Four, let's look more deeply into these symbols to understand why they have been interpreted in the manner above.

Baby: The baby referred to in this story is designated as having a particular significance in that he is to be called *Emmanuel, which means God is with us*. This birth is about a new way of understanding that God is with us (a recognized part of ourselves).

Mary: The soul deepened through devotion—intuition. To understand fully what this means, we look at the full picture of the development of the soul. Mary, the mother of Jesus, in particular, represents the soul as it magnifies the Lord through daily devotion in its preparation for a higher life. It symbolizes love and initiation (transformation) through discipline and training as the deep, feminine quality of intuition is brought forth. The individual who consistently devotes time and study to spiritual principles eventually develops a quiet nature that births the deep voice of intuition.

In Hebrew, Mary means *contradiction and bitterness*. Often, what comes through intuitively can be a bitter pill to swallow because it contradicts the ideas and beliefs one is raised with: dysfunctional rules, irrational belief systems, and dogma that no longer makes sense. Thus, the full definition of Mary is the deep unconditional love and devotion of the soul that deepens into intuitive knowing.

Joseph: Joseph is Hebrew for *whom Jehovah (God) will add it, increase progressively*. This refers to the faculty within man that triggers increase, which is the imagination. It is the quality that continually grows, expands, and increases in character. Thus, Joseph can be a symbol of the imagination: the imaging, increasing power of the mind.

Angel: Angel is Greek for *messenger of God*. Our angels are our *spiritual perceptive faculties*, which ever dwell in the presence of the Father (God). *I assure you, their angels in heaven constantly behold my Father's face.* Matthew 18:1010

Step Four: Conclusion - Initially, there was shame and denial, then acceptance regarding a new beginning relative to the awareness that God is with us. Joseph (imagination) was engaged (committed) to Mary (intuition), but they had not yet married (united). Through the faculties of imagination and intuition there was to be a new beginning (baby), which involved the idea that God is within. Mary (intuition) was great with child (ready to birth this new way). Joseph (imagination) was of the mind to put intuition away quietly. This means that, even though we have the imagination and desire for increase, we may not be willing to trust our intuition. It is by following intuition that growth takes place and we understand that God is within. Joseph (imagination) was not quite ready (aligned) to commit to Mary (intuition) and considered disclaiming it.

But a messenger from God (angel) intercedes, instructing our imagination faculty to accept intuitive knowing because this new way (baby) is born of the Holy Spirit. (It is the way of God.) This new way is to be a son (aggressive energy) of the Father (God) and will save us from error (sin). This is as the prophet (wise ones) have said. Imagination follows intuition and fulfills the spiritual process.

Summing it up, there is a new way being born or coming into existence within our awareness. It is a result of study and devotion to develop intuition. It directs the imagination from the desire for increase. It is through the merging or aligning of these two faculties that we begin to understand that God is within. As we develop our communion with God (within), we are saved from error, confusion, and misinterpretation.

There can be hesitation in grasping and taking responsibility for this new way because of our inexperience in understanding the process of spiritual unfoldment. But we receive the angelic impulse (message) from God (Higher Self) to accept this new way and, thus, we go forward with it. A complete unification of intuition and imagination is not available until this new way has been manifested into our physical experience, i.e., until we agree with it. All of this follows the predicted process of spiritual unfoldment.

Synopsis

- There are references to hidden wisdom in the Bible. You are instructed to seek beyond literal translations of the words to discover deeper meanings. This requires looking with different eyes and listening with receptive ears.
- The Bible and other holy books speak in allegory, parables, and symbols, which can easily be interpreted to provide personal meaning.
- First, look at stories and events as not only historical, but as experiences within the self. Ask questions to evoke answers that help you see with new eyes. By remaining open, you discover that the stories illustrate stages in your own personal evolution.
- Second, view the names of people in the Bible as clues to what each represents to you as far as aspects, qualities, or characteristics of self. By noting a character's expression, you delineate the quality it references. The Hebrew, Greek, or Arabic meanings of the name also supply insight.
- Third, names of places are also symbolic and refer to states of consciousness.
- Fourth, numbers play a significant role in interpretation. Note the symbolism of numbers in the list of dream symbols.
- Fifth, look for key words as symbols.
- Sixth, have fun with the process. It is joyful to recognize the text has higher meanings and much to teach. Be careful not to get mired in detail and lose the point or message of the story. Look for the theme developed in a passage. Your intuition will help you *feel* the story.
- You will find a theme in stories and parables. Summarize each paragraph, story, or chapter to enhance the flow and arrive at a larger picture.
- Use the dream interpretation Four-Step Formula to unlock biblical meanings to significance that will aid in your growth.

Chapter 12

The Symbolism of the Bhagavad Gita

It is better to live your own destiny imperfectly than to live an imitation of somebody else's life with perfection.
The mind is restless and difficult of restrain, but it is subdued by practice.
Bhagavad Gita

The Bhagavad Gita, also called *The Message of the Master* or *The Song of the Lord*, is a book compiled and adapted from various translations of original Sanskrit text. The *Gita*, as it is called, is very popular among the Hindu people and is considered a great authority regarding doctrine. Its teachings blend the varying points of Patanjali, Kapila, and the Vedas. There are many translations of the original text, but the same meaning carries through all of them.

To read and understand this poem, "The Song of the Lord," beyond the outer presentation or words on paper, allows the reader to access great esoteric teachings. Like the Bible, the Gita's text can be read in layers so that each person can carry from it personal understandings. Studying it can help one *see* symbolism in yet another context. To read it any other way is a great loss.

The dialogue, in the text, occurs between Krishna (Highest Consciousness or Divine Self) and Prince Arjuna (the conscious mind trying to understand the dilemma of life). The story unfolds on a battlefield on the brink of a war that Arjuna does not want to fight.

As they discuss the battle that unfolds before them, the conflict mirrors the internal war within Arjuna and each person. It represents the struggle for self-mastery that each must wage. There are many truths spoken during this conversation and a multitude of lessons to be derived. The entire text is written in symbolic language, yet readily understandable if you recognize that it is written to address man's inner turmoil.

Krishna (Divine Self) stands with Arjuna (individual, conscious self) observing the field of battle that spreads out before them. The struggle is between various forces vying for man's attention. There are the material symbols of earth life, the five senses that attempt to inform consciousness as to what is important and what is seen to be happening, and the inner original essence that observes and speaks for another reality.

As the story progresses, there is a lengthy struggle and brief war between two sides of the Bharata family, the Pandavas and the Kauravas, over their kingdom of Hastinapura. The battle has to do with the field of dharma (moral standing or life purpose). It lays out a dialogue between the Pandava warrior, Arjuna, and his charioteer and trusted advisor, Krishna.

The Kauravas have more men, yet the Pandavas seem to have the gods' favor. This is illustrated by the fact that, even though the Kauravas have mighty conch horns, the Pandava horns are divine and shake the earth and sky. (Here, you get a sense of supreme power or higher power with the Pandavas.) The Kauravas have more men, yet still operate at a deficit as the Pandavas appear to have a divine edge in the battle.

As Krishna drives Arjuna's chariot into the fray, Arjuna realizes that he cannot kill his cousins (the idea that all people are brothers) because he believes that to fight would destroy the moral standing of his family. There could be no pleasure in this victory. Thus, Arjuna lowers his weapon and weeps, feeling that he is in an impossible situation.

Krishna reprimands Arjuna for being a coward and suggests he is blind to the fundamental truth that people's souls do not die with their bodies. Rather, the eternal soul moves on and is reincarnated in another body. There is no point in grieving for his family members, but instead, he should follow his dharma as a warrior by fighting. If he wins the war, he will rule the earth. And if he loses, he will ascend to heaven. But if he refuses to fight, he disgraces himself because he had come into this life to be a warrior.

Does any of this look like you? If not, read this narrative again.

Krishna further states that people can let go of their attachment to the fruits of their action, turn away from the false realm of the senses, and free themselves from negative emotions by uniting with divinity. The point is to dissolve the sense of self (ego) and transcend the material world to blissfully reunite with God (Higher Reality).

Even with this small caption, the Gita holds many lessons about what one's duty really is, how one chooses to direct life, and the false messages and attachments of the senses, emotions, and rewards of action.

Every player in the story represents a part of self. The battle symbolizes man's internal and external earthly struggle. The ultimate point is to perform your duty to the best of your ability without concern for the outcome, and in so doing, you are able to rise or transcend in consciousness.

This is a sampling of the messages of the Gita. It is rich with symbolism and paves the way for a deeper understanding of the self as one evolves through earth life.

Synopsis

- The Bhagavad Gita also called *The Message of the Master,* is a book or poem compiled and adapted from various translations of original Sanskrit text.
- To understand the Gita beyond the outer presentation or words on paper allows the reader to access great esoteric teachings. It can be read in layers, allowing each person to receive a personal understanding.
- Studying the Gita can help one *see* symbolism in another context. To read it any other way loses its rich value.
- The text represents a dialogue between the Divine Self and the conscious mind, which attempts to understand the battle or the dilemma of life. The conflict is between the physical self, five senses, emotions, and intuitive knowing.

Chapter 13

Lucid Dreaming – What It Is and How to Do It

Lucid dreaming happens when you are conscious during a dream. This typically occurs during REM (Rapid Eye Movement) sleep. REM indicates that you are in a dream state.

In sleep studies, it has been proven that when the dreamer is in REM sleep, he is dreaming. If the dreamer is awakened during this part of sleep and not allowed to be in REM for a long period, he becomes anxious and disjointed. This is because, during REM sleep, we process our day. We *need* this time to put things in order and have clarity about where we go from where we are.

Often, lucid dreaming will happen spontaneously. But that doesn't mean you have to wait for that to happen. There are techniques that can be used to induce lucid dreaming.

Because dreams are therapeutic, learning how to cause them can offer great healing potential. In effect, if you were to travel into a past trauma and observe the event without getting hooked by it, you very possibly could learn things about yourself that could alter the way you deal with future upsetting events or traumas. Psychophysiology's Doctor Stephen LaBerge has found that using lucid dreaming methods can assist patients in healing from trauma, including Post Traumatic Stress Disorder and anxiety.

The mind does not know the difference between a real or imagined experience. By relaxing, letting the mind drift, then creating a dream-event, you can easily slip into lucid dreaming. The trick is to keep one part of your body uncomfortable, like sitting on your leg or keeping your body at an angle that is a bit uncomfortable, just a bit. That way, you don't go all the way into the dream state. It will allow you to maintain some awake consciousness while you enter lucid dreaming.

This process could be an imaginary dream-event, like walking into an Indian village and meeting a Shaman. As you visualize this event and *feel* it fully, you let go of other thoughts and allow the mind to take you where it will.

You can limit the time you stay in this state by setting a timer. You don't want to slip all the way into a ninety-minute dream. When you get good at this process, you can reconstruct a past experience, if you wish, for the purpose of understanding it fully. Also, as you get better at this form of mind control, you can alter the event as you see fit. This is a way to practice being in control of your emotions and attitudes, at least to the degree that you are able to, as you move through life.

You can create a dream-event that has the potential for any outcome you desire. As you *dream* the ending or outcome, it will be imprinted in your subconscious mind. Again, the subconscious does not know the difference between a real or imagined experience. But it does know how to bring about your imagined result. This process allows you to set up a new or renewed outcome and heal an experience.

To restate this: you have the ability to observe the life you are living in the same way that you observe a dream. Learning how to do this brings tremendous objectivity and the ability to remain centered, no matter what is going on. Here are the steps.

1. Decide ahead of time what scene you are going to create. Place your body in a position to relax, but not too deeply. Sit a little crooked or fold your leg beneath you. Let yourself be a little uncomfortable to make sure you stay conscious.

2. Set a time for five to ten minutes.

3. Relax, close your eyes, and create your dream scenario. Observe without attachment. Let it unfold naturally. If you are working with an event in order to change the outcome, walk into the subconscious by using a natural setting: the woods, a park, a shining sun, a beautiful lake. Then, switch the scene to the event you want to alter.

4. When the timer goes off or when you feel complete in your dream experience, write down all the details you can remember: who, what, when, where,

how, etc.

In time, you will perfect your methodology. Keep practicing. Your desired results probably won't happen overnight, but they will happen if you are patient and consistent.

Synopsis

- Lucid dreaming happens when you are conscious during a dream.
- In sleep studies, it has been proven that when the dreamer is in REM sleep, he is dreaming.
- Dreams can be therapeutic. Learning how to create them can offer healing potential, such as working through traumatic experiences.
- You can evoke a lucid dream and, through it, learn to manage your mind and thoughts.
- Learning how to create lucid dreams can help you develop keen observation skills while awake.
- There are steps you can take to master lucid dreaming.

Chapter 14

Conclusion – Where Do You Go from Here?

The Universe is always speaking to us. We must learn to listen.
Buckminster Fuller

We live in a dream reality, which is why symbols are so important. As each of us chooses awareness, we must examine our own consciousness. That means that whatever we face and deal with belongs to us. There is no running from the reality we have created. If we are angry, we face anger in the situations and people in our lives. If we are harmonious, we gravitate toward others who are harmonious. Struggle begets more struggle. Fear mirrors fear. Peace precipitates peace. Everything shows up as symbols of our state of being. There are no accidents.

In this book, I have illustrated the importance of dreams as tools for personal assessment and growth. Through dreams, each has at hand a wonderful resource to understand oneself and one's life. Utilizing dream symbolism in everyday situations clarifies lessons and messages from the Universe. Symbols, thus, can become shortcuts to communication that hastens awareness. When an owl hoots, we can know *wisdom* is at hand. When threatened by a tornado, we can look to see what element in our lives is *swirling*, possibly *out of control*. When confronted with rancor, we might ask: "What inside of me is out of sorts?" These are the type of questions that illuminate our lives as projections of what we are to learn. We can discover what is truth, what is misunderstood, and what are our false conclusions. From there, we can make adjustments, forgive, elevate our understanding, and grow.

The mind is a marvelous mechanism. It is said that we use but a tiny portion of our brain power and thus a tiny bit of our potential. Fortunately, we have unlimited capacity when we graduate to higher awareness. More is always possible. By directing the mind with discrimination and asking deeper questions, we can begin to comprehend what is possible. We begin to recognize that we are living in a larger reality than previously thought. As we mature, answers come more easily and intuition is heightened. With this development, situations are more easily discernable. Answers come, our connection expands, confidence grows, and we are more at peace.

Yes, it is true that the Universe is always talking to you. You are continually guided. The goal in this book is to help you dialogue with it. To do so, you must look beyond the limited world of form and identify your personal messages and lessons. Examining family and work dynamics help to label what is relevant. You will begin to acknowledge that each person plays a part in your growth and you in theirs. This promotes healing and freedom.

By acknowledging the symbolism life offers, you begin to appreciate who you are and what is possible. You learn to "read" your circumstances and have a better grasp on deciding what to do next and how you want to develop. You discover that all you need to do to transform your experience is to change yourself.

We are part of a larger cosmology. Each step we take along the path of self-awareness not only helps us but adds to the consciousness of all. Together, we are one in the vast Quantum Network. As one person wakes up, there is new light shining for all.

Dream work leads to deepest knowing. As an educated observer, you will see nuances unavailable before. You will be able to distinguish cause and understand why things are as they are, along with what to do next.

By incorporating the methods in this book, you become more attentive to the details and feelings of your world. You deal with life more honestly, and your inner self is stabilized. As your sixth (psychic) sense becomes operable, you tune in easily to people and situations. It simplifies problem solving. There is so much to learn and cultivate. Life is indeed an exciting adventure!

I give this information on dreams and symbolism with my blessings. I have been greatly rewarded by learning this inner language, and I know that you will find yourself expanded by its use as well.

Dream Worksheets

Capture Your Dreams Here

Refer to the Four-Step Formula and the sample dreams for reference.

Date:

Dream:

Step One – Feelings:

Step Two – Theme:

Step Three – Symbols:

Step Four – Conclusion:

How does this interpretation relate to your activities and feelings yesterday? How does it relate to your life?

Date:

Dream:

Step One – Feelings:

Step Two – Theme:

Step Three – Symbols:

Step Four – Conclusion:

How does this interpretation relate to your activities and feelings yesterday? How does it relate to your life?

Date:

Dream:

Step One – Feelings:

Step Two – Theme:

Step Three – Symbols:

Step Four – Conclusion:

How does this interpretation relate to your activities and feelings yesterday? How does it relate to your life?

Date:

Dream:

Step One – Feelings:

Step Two – Theme:

Step Three – Symbols:

Step Four – Conclusion:

How does this interpretation relate to your activities and feelings yesterday? How does it relate to your life?

Date:

Dream:

Step One – Feelings:

Step Two – Theme:

Step Three – Symbols:

Step Four – Conclusion:

How does this interpretation relate to your activities and feelings yesterday? How does it relate to your life?

Date:

Dream:

Step One – Feelings:

Step Two – Theme:

Step Three – Symbols:

Step Four – Conclusion:

How does this interpretation relate to your activities and feelings yesterday? How does it relate to your life?

Date:

Dream:

Step One – Feelings:

Step Two – Theme:

Step Three – Symbols:

Step Four – Conclusion:

How does this interpretation relate to your activities and feelings yesterday? How does it relate to your life?

About Jean Walters

Jean Walters is a St. Louis based teacher of Self-Empowerment principles. She has been in the field of personal growth for forty years, has studied metaphysics extensively, and applies Universal principles to every area of her life.

In her practice, she helps clients sort through relationships, career choices, experiences, decisions, lessons to learn, and a path to follow. Along the way, she has developed classes, books, and videos to educate students and truth seekers in universal law, meditation, dreams and their value, the practicality of personal growth, and various personal-empowerment methods to develop spiritually.

During her career, she has written nine books, published numerous free-lance articles, as well as written weekly and monthly columns in major newspapers and publications. Her syndicated radio show, *Positive Moments*, was broadcast on 110 stations around the nation. She has been a featured guest on radio, television, and podcasts. Additionally, Walters has lectured, designed, and taught classes and workshops for many organizations, colleges, universities and businesses.

Presently, she has a private practice as a Transformational Coach in St. Louis, Missouri. Her personal-growth classes are taught at various locations, including the St. Louis Community College. Also, for over thirty years, she has provided over 35,000 Akashic (psychic) readings to those seeking personal insight concerning life-purpose, relationships, health, career, and various other dynamics of life.

Her Mission Statement: To encourage, assist, and guide individuals to live freely and express from their Highest Selves.

Check out Jean's resources:

Website:

http://www.spiritualtransformation.com

Blog:

http://www.spiritualtransformation.com/blog

Amazon.com author page:

https://www.amazon.com/Jean-Walters/e/B00MGBVDJS/

Video library:

https://www.youtube.com/channel/UCnVjf1AAnzZxi56reIkif3g

https://www.youtube.com/channel/UCroNsq_NFvpiiG8bJa44Kyg

Meditation Class:

https://www.udemy.com/course/the-art-of-meditation-how-and-why

Newsletter: (specials, information on upcoming classes and inspirational pick-me-ups. YES YOU CAN articles, and other interesting tidbits):

http://www.spiritualtransformation.com/subscribe.php

Email Address (for questions or more information):

jean@spiritualtransformation.com

Other Books Written by Jean Walters

Set Yourself Free: *Live the Life YOU Were Meant to Live*

Be Outrageous*: Do the Impossible – Others have and you can too! (Live Your Passion)*

The Power of KNOWING: *8 Step Guide to Open Your Intuitive Channel and Live in Highest Consciousness*

The Journey from Anxiety to Peace: *Practical Steps to Handle Fear, Embrace Struggle and Eliminate Worry to Become Happy and Free*

Look Mom, I'm Flying *(For children and the child within you)*

Dream Journal

Choosing Health: *You have a right to health; are you willing to claim it!*

Made in the USA
Monee, IL
07 January 2021